MOVIE ★ ICONS

WELLES

EDITOR
PAUL DUNCAN

TEXT
F. X. FEENEY

PHOTOS
THE KOBAL COLLECTION

TASCHEN

HONG KONG KÖLN LONDON LOS ANGELES MADRID PARIS TOKYO

CONTENTS

1

ORSON WELLES: JOYOUS CREATION

BY F.X. FEENEY

ORSON WELLES: FROHES SCHAFFEN

ORSON WELLES : UNE JOYEUSE CRÉATIVITÉ

ORSON WELLES: JOYOUS CREATION

by F. X. Feeney

In the beginning, there was that God-like voice.

"This is Orson Welles," he would intone. His earliest audience was America in the dark heart of the 1930s. His medium was radio. President Franklin D. Roosevelt also thrived then, using *his* great voice to console poverty-stricken Americans about their plight and to warn of tyrants marching their armies throughout Europe and Asia.

Welles took a keen interest in such events. He and theater producer John Houseman triumphantly staged an all-black *Macbeth* (an answer to 1930s racism), *Julius Caesar* (styled to evoke Hitler and Mussolini) and *Faust* (tricked out as an enormous magic act, with levitations and vanishings). When they adapted H.G. Wells' *War of the Worlds* for radio in 1938, their format of an on-the-spot newscast was so effective that, of the seven million people listening, a million and a half took action against what they naïvely believed was an actual invasion from Mars.

Roosevelt was alarmed. Nevertheless he took a personal liking to Welles, and encouraged him to consider a career in politics. Welles heeded this, even as Hollywood beckoned. For all its freewheeling exuberance, his first (and most agree, greatest) film *Citizen Kane* (1941) is nothing if not a stealthy commercial for Welles as a thinker and potential leader. That it also pricked the ego of newspaper tycoon William Randolph Hearst made Welles himself a political lightning rod. His Hollywood career promptly capsized. His partnership with Houseman crashed and burned. His poetic family saga *The Magnificent Ambersons* (1942) was butchered on the editing table. After Roosevelt's death, Welles was as much an outcast in Washington as Hollywood – and so began his long, nomadic later career as an independent filmmaker, which he supported by working as an actor in hundreds of films, radio plays, TV shows and even (later in life) wine commercials. He recited Shakespeare wherever he was asked, most comically with

ON THE SET OF 'CITIZEN KANE' (1941)
Action! Aided by great cameraman Gregg Toland
(seated). / Action! Mit Unterstützung des großen Kame-
ramanns Gregg Toland (sitzend). / Moteur ! Secondé
par le grand chef opérateur Gregg Toland (assis).

"He was some kind of a man.
What does it matter what you say about people?"
Tanya, 'Touch of Evil'

ON THE SET OF 'CITIZEN KANE' (1941)
Dynamic, observant energy personified. / Immer ein dynamischer, energiegeladener Beobachter. / Un condensé d'énergie, dynamique et attentif à la fois.

Lucille Ball as Juliet in a famous episode of *I Love Lucy*, and, most movingly as Shylock, seemingly off the cuff (clean-shaven and in a Vegas tuxedo) on Dean Martin's variety show in 1967. "I began at the top and worked my way down," he often joked – a shrewd defense against anyone beating him to *that* punch line. By the night of his death at age 70 in 1985, he was unjustly mantled in a mystique of failure.

In the years since, it has become clear Welles used the loot from his workaday outings to finance a string of increasingly passionate, beautifully realized films. *Lady from Shanghai* (1948) *Othello* (1952), *Mr Arkadin* (1955), *The Trial* (1962), *The Immortal Story* (1967) and *F for Fake* (1974) each suffered from a shortage of funds, battles with backers, the poverty of distributors and the myopia of critics, but each sings with Welles' energy and joyous creation, and they rightfully take their places beside *Citizen Kane*. Welles is like the great juggler who, if he drops the ball, makes it look like part of the act. In times to come, I am sure we will see more (and better versions) of his *Don Quixote*, *The Other Side of the Wind* and *The Deep* – bits of these unfinished films continue to surface around the world like fossils and flint arrowheads.

When he overacts, Welles reveals the layers of obsession and self-doubt that drive life's overactors, but it is a different story when a director or role wins his trust. Think of *The Third*

Man (1949), *Prince of Foxes* (1948), *Compulsion* (1959) and *Ferry to Hong Kong* (1959), or those sublime performances given under his own hard eye in *Touch of Evil* (1958) and *Chimes at Midnight* (1966). Welles the actor is equal to

ON THE SET OF 'CITIZEN KANE' (1941)
Rehearsing a table filled with fellow actors. / Bei den Proben an einem Tisch voller Schauspielkollegen. / Répétition avec une tablée d'autres acteurs.

portraying the unruliest attacks on the soul. Think of that magnificent moment in *Chimes at Midnight* when Falstaff, dying inside, forgives his brutal rejection by his dearest friend and spiritual son, Prince Hal. Or see what filmmaker Henry Jaglom caught of his great friend in *Someone to Love* (1987), the last film in which the living Welles consented to appear. Both Jaglom and Welles were plainly conscious of this possibility, and make the most of it. Welles' avuncular, intelligent discussion of sexual politics in the film's last reel is a sweet, heady note on which to round out his life's work as both a performer and a political thinker. And Jaglom ends the film on an iconic view, run without sound – he lets that great voice fall violently still, in deepest tribute. The snippet shows Welles rumbling merrily in a moment of unguarded, heartfelt laughter: All forgiving, self-mocking, life loving.

ORSON WELLES: FROHES SCHAFFEN

von F. X. Feeney

Am Anfang war diese gottgleiche Stimme.

„Hier spricht Orson Welles", tönte sie. Ihre ersten Zuhörer fand sie im depressionsgeplagten Amerika der 1930er Jahre. Ihr Medium war der Rundfunk. Es war auch die Zeit von Präsident Franklin D. Roosevelt, der gleichfalls seine Stimme nutzte, um seine verarmten Mitbürger über ihr Schicksal hinwegzutrösten und gleichzeitig vor den Tyrannen zu warnen, die mit ihren Armeen durch Europa und Asien marschierten.

Welles hatte an solchen Ereignissen reges Interesse. Er und der Theaterproduzent John Houseman hatten erfolgreich einen *Macbeth* mit ausschließlich dunkelhäutigen Schauspielern auf die Bühne gebracht (als Reaktion auf den Rassismus der dreißiger Jahre), einen *Julius Caesar*, der bewusst an Hitler und Mussolini erinnerte, und einen *Faust*, der wie eine gewaltige Zaubervorstellung inszeniert war, mit Figuren, die schwebten und verschwanden. Als sie *Den Krieg der Welten* von H. G. Wells 1938 als Hörspiel präsentierten, wirkte ihr Format der Live-Berichterstattung so überzeugend, dass sich fast ein Viertel der sieben Millionen Zuhörer vor der Invasion vom Mars tatsächlich zu schützen versuchten.

Roosevelt war alarmiert. Trotzdem war ihm Welles sympathisch und er ermunterte ihn, sich politisch zu engagieren. Welles folgte diesem Rat, selbst noch als er den Lockruf Hollywoods hörte. Bei allem Überschwang ist sein erster (und nach allgemeiner Auffassung bester) Film, *Citizen Kane* (1941), vor allem ein heimlicher Werbefilm für Welles als Denker und potentieller Staatsmann. Dass er damit auch am Ego des Zeitungsmagnaten William Randolph Hearst kratzte, machte Welles selbst zum politischen Blitzableiter. Seine Hollywood-Karriere lief denn auch prompt auf Grund. Seine Partnerschaft mit Houseman ging in Rauch und Flammen auf. Seine poetische Familiensaga *Der Glanz des Hauses Amberson* (1942) wurde auf dem Schneidetisch gemetzelt. Und nach Roosevelts Tod war Welles in Washington ebenso geächtet wie in Hollywood – und so begann seine lange nomadenhafte Spätkarriere als unabhängiger Filmemacher, die er dadurch finanzierte, dass er in Hunderten von Filmen, Hörspielen, Fernsehsendungen und (später) sogar Weinwerbespots mitspielte. Bei jeder passenden Gelegenheit rezitierte er Shakespeare, besonders spaßig mit Lucille Ball als Julia in einer berühmten Folge von *I Love Lucy* (*Typisch Lucy*) und besonders bewegend 1967, scheinbar aus dem Stegreif (glatt-

PORTRAIT FROM 'THE THIRD MAN' (1949)
A dark, romantic leading man of his day. / Zu seiner Zeit gab er den dunklen, romantischen Helden. / L'un des héros ténébreux et romantiques de l'époque.

„Er war ein außergewöhnlicher Mann. Was spielt es schon für eine Rolle, was man über einen Menschen sagt?"
Tanya, *Im Zeichen des Bösen*

STILL FROM 'THE THIRD MAN' (1949)

rasiert und im Smoking), als Shylock in Dean Martins Unterhaltungssendung. „Ich hab ganz oben angefangen und mich nach unten durchgearbeitet", witzelte er oft – und nahm damit geschickt all jenen Spaßvögeln den Wind aus den Segeln, die gerade diesen Scherz auf den Lippen hatten. Als er 1985 im Alter von 70 Jahren starb, haftete ihm zu Unrecht der Nimbus des Versagers an.

Seither wurde aber immer deutlicher, dass Welles die Beute aus seinem Tagesgeschäft in eine Reihe prächtig und mit Leidenschaft inszenierter Filme investiert hatte. *Die Lady von Shanghai* (1948), *Othello* (1952), *Herr Satan persönlich* (1955), *Der Prozeß* (1962), *Stunde der Wahrheit* (1967) und *F wie Fälschung* (1974) litten allesamt unter Finanzierungsengpässen, Auseinandersetzungen mit den Geldgebern, der Armut der Verleihfirmen und der Kurzsichtigkeit der Kritiker, aber jeder dieser Filme legt für sich Zeugnis ab von der Freude und Schaffenskraft seines Schöpfers und nimmt zu Recht einen Platz neben *Citizen Kane* ein. Welles ist wie ein guter Jongleur, der einen Ball fallen lässt und dann so tut, als sei es Teil der Nummer. In Zukunft werden wir sicherlich noch weitere (und bessere) Fassungen seiner unvollendeten Filme *Don Quixote*, *The Other Side of the Wind* und *The Deep* sehen, denn Fragmente dieser Werke tauchen mit schöner Regelmäßigkeit in allen Ecken der Welt auf wie Fossilien oder steinzeitliche Pfeilspitzen.

Wenn er beim Schauspielen übertrieb, zeigte Welles jene Besessenheit und jene Selbstzweifel, die alle Über-Schauspieler antreiben, aber wenn ein Regisseur oder eine Rolle einmal sein Vertrauen

gewonnen hatten, sah es ganz anders aus. Man denke nur an *Der dritte Mann* (1949), *In den Klauen des Borgia* (1948), *Der Zwang zum Bösen* (1959) und *Fähre nach Hongkong* (1959) oder an jene hervorragenden Leistungen, die er unter sei-

ON THE SET OF 'THE THIRD MAN' (1949)
Carol Reed was a great favorite of his, "a true actor's director." / Carol Reed schätzte er besonders, weil er mit Schauspielern umzugehen verstand. / Carol Reed est l'un de ses grands favoris, « un vrai directeur d'acteurs ».

nem eigenen gestrengen Auge in *Im Zeichen des Bösen* (1958) und *Falstaff* (1966) bot. Der Schauspieler Welles war in der Lage, die ungestümsten Angriffe auf die Seele darzustellen. Man erinnere sich an jenen herrlichen Augenblick in *Falstaff*, als dieser, innerlich sterbend, Vergebung findet für die brutale Zurückweisung durch seinen engsten Freund und geistigen Sohn, Prinz Hal. Oder man schaue sich an, was der Filmemacher Henry Jaglom aus seinem großen Freund in *Ein Tag für die Liebe* (1987) heraus-holte; es ist der letzte Film, in dem der lebende Welles aus freier Entscheidung auftrat. Sowohl Jaglom als auch Welles waren sich dessen vollkommen bewusst und machten das Beste daraus. Welles' onkel-hafte, intelligente Diskussion der Sexualpolitik im letzten Teil des Films ist ein liebenswerter, berau-schender Schlussakkord zur Abrundung seines Lebenswerks, sei es als Darsteller oder auch als politi-scher Denker. Und Jaglom beendet den Film mit einer symbolischen Einstellung, die ohne Ton läuft: Er lässt diese große Stimme einfach verstummen, als Zeichen größter Hochachtung. Diese Sequenz zeigt einen fröhlich knurrenden Welles in einem Augenblick ungezügelten, herzlichen Gelächters - jemand, der alles vergibt, über sich selbst lachen kann und das Leben liebt.

ORSON WELLES : UNE JOYEUSE CRÉATIVITÉ

F. X. Feeney

Au commencement, il y a cette voix caverneuse digne de Dieu le Père.

« Ici Orson Welles », entonne-t-il. Son premier public sera l'Amérique des heures sombres des années 1930. Son support est la radio. C'est également l'heure de gloire du président Franklin Roosevelt, dont la voix tout aussi légendaire console les Américains réduits à la misère et les met en garde contre les tyrans qui déploient leurs armées à travers l'Europe et l'Asie.

Welles s'intéresse vivement à ces événements. Avec le producteur de théâtre John Houseman, il monte triomphalement une version de *Macbeth* jouée par des acteurs noirs (en réponse au racisme de l'époque), un *Jules César* évoquant Hitler et Mussolini et un *Faust* transformé en immense tour de magie, avec lévitation et tours de passe-passe à l'appui. Lorsqu'ils adaptent *La Guerre des mondes* de H. G. Wells à la radio en 1938, ils créent si bien l'illusion d'un bulletin d'information relatant l'événement en direct que sur les sept millions d'auditeurs qui le suivent, un million et demi de personnes réagissent à ce qu'elles prennent naïvement pour une véritable invasion de Martiens.

Roosevelt est alarmé. Il se prend néanmoins d'affection pour Orson Welles et l'incite à envisager une carrière politique. Bien que Hollywood lui tende les bras, Welles n'est pas sourd à ces conseils. Malgré son exubérance débridée, son premier film (que la plupart s'accordent à considérer comme le meilleur), *Citizen Kane* (1941), n'est autre qu'une publicité masquée pour les qualités de penseur et de leader du metteur en scène. Hélas, le film froisse la susceptibilité du magnat de la presse William Randolph Hearst, qui le fera payer cher à Orson Welles. Sa carrière hollywoodienne ne tarde pas à capoter. Son partenariat avec Houseman se désagrège. Sa saga familiale et poétique, *La Splendeur des Amberson* (1942), est charcutée sur la table de montage. Après la mort de Roosevelt, Welles devient un paria à Washington comme à Hollywood. C'est ainsi que débute sa longue carrière nomade de cinéaste indépendant, qu'il finance en se produisant comme acteur dans des centaines de films, de pièces radiophoniques et d'émissions télévisées, voire dans des publicités pour du vin. Il déclame du Shakespeare à la demande, l'exemple le plus comique étant un célèbre épisode de la série *I Love Lucy*,

ON THE SET OF 'CITIZEN KANE' (1941)

« C'était un sacré bonhomme. Qu'importe ce qu'on dit des gens ? »
Tanya, *La Soif du mal*

ON THE SET OF 'THE LADY FROM
SHANGHAI' (1948)

avec Lucille Ball dans le rôle de Juliette, tandis que son interprétation la plus émouvante reste celle de Shylock, apparemment à l'improviste (il est rasé de près et vêtu d'un smoking rutilant) dans l'émission de variétés de Dean Martin, en 1967. « J'ai démarré au sommet et je suis descendu à la force du poignet », dit-il souvent en guise de plaisanterie, devançant ainsi toutes les critiques susceptibles d'aller dans ce sens. Lorsqu'il décède en 1985 à l'âge de 70 ans, une image de raté lui colle injustement à la peau.

Depuis lors, il est devenu évident qu'Orson Welles a utilisé le butin de ses emplois alimentaires pour financer une série de films toujours plus passionnés et magnifiquement réalisés. *La Dame de Shanghaï* (1948), *Othello* (1952), *Dossier secret* (1955), *Le Procès* (1962), *Une histoire immortelle* (1967) et *Vérité et mensonges* (1974) ont tous souffert du manque de moyens, des conflits avec les producteurs, de l'indigence des distributeurs et de la myopie des critiques, mais tous brillent de l'éclat et de la joyeuse créativité d'Orson Welles et méritent pleinement leur place aux côtés de *Citizen Kane*. Welles est comme ces grands jongleurs qui, s'ils laissent tomber une balle, parviennent à donner l'impression que cela fait partie du spectacle. À l'avenir, je suis convaincu que nous découvrirons de nouveaux extraits (et de meilleures versions) de *Don Quixote*, de *The Other Side of the Wind* et de *The Deep*, œuvres inachevées dont des fragments continuent à être exhumés aux quatre coins du monde tels des fossiles et des flèches de silex.

Lorsqu'il surjoue, Welles révèle l'amas d'obsessions et de doutes dont souffrent ceux qui en font trop dans la vie comme à l'écran, mais il en va différemment lorsqu'un metteur en scène ou un rôle parvient à gagner sa confiance. Prenez *Le Troisième Homme* (1949), *Échec à Borgia* (1948), *Le Génie du mal* (1959) et *Visa pour Hong-Kong* (1959), ou encore les sublimes interprétations qu'il livre à sa propre caméra dans *La Soif du mal* (1958) et *Falstaff* (1966). Welles l'acteur s'attache à dépeindre les plus violents déchirements de l'âme. Souvenez-vous de cette scène magnifique de *Falstaff* où le héros, mort intérieurement, pardonne son reniement brutal à son fils spirituel, le prince Hal. Ou voyez ce que le réalisateur Henry Jaglom a saisi de son grand ami dans *Someone to Love* (1987), le dernier film où Welles a consenti à apparaître de son vivant. Manifestement conscients qu'il s'agit sans doute là d'un adieu, Jaglom et Welles en tirent pleinement parti. Les propos éclairés et sages de Welles concernant la sexualité dans la dernière bobine concluent sur une note douce et grisante sa carrière d'artiste et de penseur. Jaglom termine le film sur une image symbolique projetée sans le son, laissant cette formidable voix se taire brutalement en guise d'hommage. Ce finale nous montre Orson Welles secoué par un grand éclat de rire spontané et sincère, exprimant à la fois son pardon, son autodérision et son amour de la vie.

PAGE 22
**STAGE PRODUCTION 'HEARTBREAK HOUSE'
(1938)**
Welles as Captain Shotover in George Bernard Shaw's play, with Geraldine Fitzgerald as Ellie Dunn. / Welles als Kapitän Shotover in George Bernard Shaws Schauspiel, mit Geraldine Fitzgerald als Ellie Dunn. / Welles en capitaine Shotover dans la pièce de George Bernard Shaw, avec Geraldine Fitzgerald dans le rôle d'Ellie Dunn.

2

VISUAL FILMOGRAPHY

FILMOGRAFIE IN BILDERN
FILMOGRAPHIE EN IMAGES

FAME

RUHM

LA CÉLÉBRITÉ

RADIO BROADCAST
Welles wrote, directed and performed for CBS radio from 1936. / Welles schrieb, inszenierte und spielte ab 1936 Hörspiele für CBS. / À partir de 1936, Welles écrit, réalise et interprète des pièces radiophoniques pour CBS Radio.

PAGES 24/25
STAGE PRODUCTION 'JULIUS CAESAR' (1937)
His inward Brutus hints at how Welles might have played Hamlet. / Sein in sich gekehrter Brutus lässt ahnen, wie Welles Hamlet gespielt hätte. / Son Brutus introverti laisse deviner comment Welles aurait joué Hamlet.

RADIO BROADCAST
Welles became world-famous when his broadcast of H.G. Wells' 'The War of the Worlds' on 30 October 1938 caused widespread panic. / Welles gelangte zu Weltruhm, als sein Hörspiel nach H. G. Wells' Der Krieg der Welten bei der Ausstrahlung am 30. Oktober 1938 vielerorts Panik auslöste. / Welles devient mondialement célèbre le 30 octobre 1938, lorsque la diffusion de La Guerre des mondes de H. G. Wells provoque une panique générale.

ORSON WELLES
in
JOHN CITIZEN, U. S. A.
and
ONE OTHER PRODUCTION

"I am supposed to be an innovator, and I have quietly given myself a few bows for all of those things that it turns out I didn't invent. I did invent, but my big inventions were in radio and theatre. Much more than in movies."
Orson Welles, 'This is Orson Welles'

„Es heißt, dass ich ein großer Neuerer sei, und ich hab mir auch schon heimlich auf die Schultern geklopft für all diese Dinge, die ich dann, wie sich am Ende herausgestellt hat, doch nicht erfunden habe. Ich habe erfunden, aber meine großen Erfindungen waren im Rundfunk und auf der Bühne, viel weniger im Kino."
Orson Welles, This is Orson Welles

« Je suis censé être un novateur et je me suis discrètement donné quelques coups de chapeau pour toutes les choses qu'il s'avère que je n'ai pas inventées. J'ai réellement été un inventeur, mais mes principales inventions concernent la radio et le théâtre. Bien plus que le cinéma. »
Orson Welles, This is Orson Welles

"Understudies, stage managers, cripples, children and dependants... Orson led them with an authority that was extraordinary in a boy just out of his teens. He had the strength; but he also had the infinite and loving patience which, in my experience, distinguishes the great from the competent director."
John Houseman, 'Run-Through'

„Zweitbesetzungen, Inspizienten, Krüppel, Kinder und Angehörige ... Orson führte sie mit einer Autorität, die außergewöhnlich war für einen Jungen, der gerade mal volljährig geworden war. Er besaß die Kraft, aber auch die unendliche und liebevolle Geduld, die nach meiner Erfahrung einen großen von einem gerade mal fähigen Regisseur unterscheidet."
John Houseman, Run-Through

« Les doublures, les régisseurs, les infirmes, les enfants, les personnes à charge... Orson les dirigeait avec une autorité incroyable pour un garçon d'une vingtaine d'années. Il en avait la force, mais aussi la patience infinie qui, d'après mon expérience, distingue le grand cinéaste du réalisateur compétent. »
John Houseman, Run-Through

PAGE 30
MAKE-UP TEST FOR 'CITIZEN KANE' (1941)
Welles was a cartoonist since boyhood, with ink and pen ever at the ready. / Welles war von frühester Jugend an Cartoonist und hielt Zeichenstift und Tusche stets griffbereit. / Dessinateur de bandes dessinées depuis l'enfance, Welles a toujours une plume et de l'encre à portée de main.

ADVERT FOR 'CITIZEN KANE' (1941)
An early announcement gave the film a different title. / In dieser frühen Ankündigung hatte der Film noch einen anderen Titel. / Le film est d'abord annoncé sous un autre titre.

PAGE 31
MAKE-UP TEST FOR 'CITIZEN KANE' (1941)
Welles read a book a day throughout his life. / Welles las sein Leben lang jeden Tag ein ganzes Buch. / Toute sa vie, Welles lira un livre par jour.

An Elaborate Production of the Weird Drama
DR. JEKYLL and MR. HYDE
JAS. H. WALLICK
and his FAMOUS ACTING HORSE
ROBIN CHARGER in THE BANDIT KING

STILL FROM 'CITIZEN KANE' (1941)
Composing an idealistic "declaration of principles" by gaslight. / Beim Verfassen einer idealistischen „Prinzipienerklärung" im Schein einer Gaslampe. / Kanes en train de composer une « déclaration de principes » idéaliste à la lumière du gaz.

STILL FROM 'CITIZEN KANE' (1941)
"Surprised" by a song in his honor, yet – he knows all the words! / „Überrascht" von einem Lied zu seinen Ehren – trotzdem kennt er den gesamten Text! / Kanes « surpris » par une chanson en son honneur dont il connaît pourtant toutes les paroles !

**PRODUCTION SKETCH FOR 'CITIZEN KANE'
BY CLAUDE GILLINGWATER, JR (1941)**
The fractured narrative required careful planning of
every scene. / Produktionsskizze von Claude
Gillingwater, Jr.: Die gebrochene Erzählweise verlangte,
dass jede Szene sorgfältig geplant wurde. / Croquis de
Claude Gillingwater, Jr. Le récit fractionné nécessite
une préparation minutieuse de chaque scène.

PAGES 34 & 35
STILLS FROM 'CITIZEN KANE' (1941)
Greatness is in Kane's grasp (left) until scandal steals
it away (right). / Der Ruhm ist für Kane zum Greifen nah
(links), bis ein Skandal seine Pläne zunichte macht
(rechts). / Kane réalise ses rêves de grandeur
(à gauche) jusqu'à ce que le scandale arrive (à droite).

STILL FROM 'CITIZEN KANE' (1941)
Xanadu as it appeared on screen. Reporter Jerry
Thompson (William Alland) tries to find out if Raymond
(Paul Stewart) knows the meaning of "Rosebud." /
So erschien Xanadu auf der Leinwand. Reporter Jerry
Thompson (William Alland) versucht herauszufinden,
ob Raymond (Paul Stewart) die Bedeutung des Wortes
„Rosebud" kennt. / Xanadu tel qu'il apparaît à l'écran.
Le journaliste Jerry Thompson (William Alland) cherche
à savoir si Raymond (Paul Stewart) connaît la
signification du mot « Rosebud ».

PAGES 38/39
ON THE SET OF 'CITIZEN KANE' (1941)
Guiding Dorothy Commingore, despite a sprained
ankle. / Trotz eines verstauchten Knöchels führt er
Dorothy Commingore. / Malgré son entorse à la
cheville, Welles dirige Dorothy Commingore.

STILLS FROM 'CITIZEN KANE' (1941)

Top: As Kane dies he whispers "Rosebud." Bottom: We eventually find his sledge, which represents the last time Charles Foster Kane was happy. / Oben: Im Sterben flüstert Kane das Wort „Rosebud". Unten: Schließlich sieht man seinen Schlitten, der für den letzten Augenblick steht, in dem Charles Foster Kane glücklich war. / En haut : en mourant, Kane murmure le mot « Rosebud ». En bas : nous découvrons finalement son traîneau, symbole de ses derniers instants de bonheur.

STILL FROM 'CITIZEN KANE' (1941)

Right: During a flashback we see the moment when he was separated from his mother. / Rechts: In einer Rückblende sieht der Zuschauer, wie Kane von seiner Mutter getrennt wurde. / Ci-contre : un flash-back nous montre le moment où il est séparé de sa mère.

PREMIERE OF 'CITIZEN KANE' (1941)
New York Premiere at the RKO Palace on Broadway,
1 May 1941. The billboard evokes both King Kong and da
Vinci's image of man. / Die New Yorker Premiere im
RKO Palace am Broadway, 1. Mai 1941. Das Kinoplakat
erinnert sowohl an King Kong als auch an Leonardo da
Vincis Vitruvianischen Menschen. / Première new-
yorkaise au RKO Palace de Broadway, le 1ᵉʳ mai 1941.
L'affiche évoque à la fois King Kong et le célèbre
Homme de Vitruve dessiné par Léonard de Vinci.

"There, but for the grace of God, goes God."
Herman J. Mankiewicz, said of Welles directing
'Citizen Kane'

„Nur dank der Gnade Gottes geht dort nicht Gott."
Herman J. Mankiewicz über Welles, als dieser *Citizen
Kane* drehte

« Voilà, sans la grâce de Dieu, ce que Dieu ferait. »
Herman J. Mankiewicz à propos de Welles réalisant
Citizen Kane

POSTER FOR 'CITIZEN KANE' (1941)
How do you market a "multiple viewpoint" movie in
1941? / Wie vermarktet man im Jahre 1941 einen Film
mit wechselnder Erzählperspektive"? / Comment
présenter un film « polyphonique » en 1941 ?

PAGES 44/45
**STILL FROM 'THE MAGNIFICENT
AMBERSONS' (1942)**
George, possessive to his marrow, sees his mother
wooed. / George, bis ins Mark besitzergreifend, sieht
das Werben um seine Mutter. / George, possessif
jusqu'à la moelle, voit sa mère se faire courtiser.

**STILL FROM 'THE MAGNIFICENT
AMBERSONS' (1942)**
A family quarrel in a proscenium out of Shakespeare's
Globe Theatre. / Ein Familienstreit in einem Proszenium
aus Shakespeares Globe Theatre. / Querelle de famille
dans une avant-scène du Shakespeare's Globe Theatre.

*"At 21 or 22 so many things appear solid and
permanent and terrible which 40 sees are nothing
but disappearing miasma. 40 can't tell 20 about
this; 20 can find out only by getting to be 40."*
Eugene Morgan, 'The Magnificent Ambersons'

*„Mit 21 oder 22 erscheinen so viele Dinge solide
und dauerhaft und schrecklich, die man mit
vierzig als Miasma erkennt, das sich verflüchtigt.
Der Vierzigjährige kann dem Zwanzigjährigen
nichts davon erzählen. Der Zwanzigjährige kann
das nur herausfinden, indem er 40 wird."*
Eugene Morgan, *Der Glanz des Hauses Amberson*

STILL FROM 'THE MAGNIFICENT AMBERSONS' (1942)
Broke, jilted by life, Aunt Fanny (Agnes Moorehead) collapses. / Pleite und vom Leben im Stich gelassen bricht Tante Fanny (Agnes Moorehead) zusammen. / Ruinée, persécutée par le destin, tante Fanny (Agnes Moorehead) s'effondre.

« À 21 ou 22 ans, il y a tant de choses qui semblent solides, permanentes et terribles, et dont on constate à 40 ans qu'elles ne forment qu'un miasme déliquescent. Celui que nous serons à 40 ans ne peut en avertir celui que nous sommes à 20 ans. L'homme de 20 ans ne peut le découvrir qu'en atteignant 40 ans. »
Eugene Morgan, *La Splendeur des Amberson*

PAGES 48/49
ON THE SET OF 'THE MAGNIFICENT AMBERSONS' (1942)
Conferring with Tim Holt while he plots a tracking shot. / Bei der Planung einer Fahraufnahme bespricht er sich mit Tim Holt. / Conciliabule avec Tim Holt pour préparer un travelling.

"Even if I'd stayed [in the US to finish 'The
Magnificent Ambersons'] I would've had to make
compromises on the editing, but these would've
been mine and not the fruit of confused and often
semi-hysterical committees. If I had been there
myself I would have found my own solutions and
saved the picture in a form which would have
carried the stamp of my own effort."
Orson Welles, 'This is Orson Welles'

„Selbst wenn ich [in den USA] geblieben wäre,
[um Der Glanz des Hauses Amberson fertig zu
stellen,] hätte ich beim Schnitt Kompromisse
eingehen müssen, aber das wären dann meine
gewesen und nicht die Ausgeburten verwirrter und
oft halbhysterischer Ausschüsse. Wenn ich selbst
dort gewesen wäre, hätte ich meine eigenen
Lösungen gefunden und den Film in einer Form
gerettet, die den Stempel meiner eigenen Leistung
trüge."
Orson Welles, *This is Orson Welles*

« Même si j'étais resté [aux États-Unis pour finir
La Splendeur des Amberson], j'aurais dû faire des
compromis sur le montage. Mais ces compromis
auraient été les miens et non l'œuvre de comités
désorientés et semi-hystériques. Si j'avais été là en
personne, j'aurais trouvé mes propres solutions et
sauvé le film sous une forme qui aurait porté le
sceau de mes propres efforts. »
Orson Welles, *This is Orson Welles*

STILL FROM 'JOURNEY INTO FEAR' (1942)
Welles filmed this thriller by night while making 'The
Magnificent Ambersons' by day. / Welles filmte diesen
Thriller nachts, während er tagsüber *Der Glanz des
Hauses Amberson* drehte. / Welles tourne ce thriller
de nuit tout en réalisant *La Splendeur des Amberson*
de jour.

STILL FROM 'IT'S ALL TRUE' (1942)
The four Brazilian fishermen who recreated their
heroic sea journey for Welles. / Die vier brasilianischen
Fischer, die ihre heldenhafte Seereise für Welles
nachspielten. / Les quatre pêcheurs brésiliens qui ont
recréé leur épopée héroïque pour Orson Welles.

ON THE SET OF 'IT'S ALL TRUE' (1942)
Working lightly and quickly in the streets of Rio de
Janeiro. / Schnell und mit leichter Ausrüstung arbeitet
er in den Straßen von Rio de Janeiro. / Welles travaille
vite avec du matériel léger dans les rues de Rio de
Janeiro.

LEADING MAN

HAUPTROLLEN

RÔLES PRINCIPAUX

STILL FROM 'JANE EYRE' (1943)
Jane (Joan Fontaine) watches as Mr Rochester (Orson Welles), the man she loves, flirts with another woman. / Jane (Joan Fontaine) schaut zu, wie Mr. Rochester (Orson Welles), den sie liebt, mit einer anderen Frau flirtet. / Jane (Joan Fontaine) regarde Mr Rochester (Orson Welles), l'homme qu'elle aime, flirter avec une autre femme !

PAGE 54
STILL FROM 'JANE EYRE' (1943)
Finding the correct false nose for his character was part of Welles' acting process. / Die richtige falsche Nase für seine Figur zu finden, gehörte für Welles zum Schauspielen. / Trouver le faux nez approprié pour son personnage fait partie du jeu d'acteur.

"Hollywood is Hollywood. There's nothing you can say about it that isn't true, good or bad. And if you get into it, you have no right to be bitter – you're the one who sat down, and joined the game."
Orson Welles, 'The Orson Welles Story'

STILL FROM 'JANE EYRE' (1943)
Hollywood embraced Welles as a romantic star,
not as a director. / Hollywood sah Welles als Star in
romantischen Rollen, nicht als Regisseur. / Hollywood
voit en Welles une star romantique et non un metteur
en scène.

„Hollywood ist Hollywood. Man kann nichts
darüber sagen, was nicht stimmt, ob gut oder
schlecht. Und wenn man sich darauf einlässt, hat
man kein Recht, verbittert zu sein – schließlich
hat man sich ja selbst an den Tisch gesetzt und
mitgespielt."
Orson Welles, *The Orson Welles Story*

« Hollywood, c'est Hollywood. On ne peut rien
dire à son sujet qui ne soit vrai, en bien ou en mal.
Et si on y pénètre, on n'a pas le droit d'être amer :
personne ne vous a forcé à vous asseoir et à vous
joindre à la partie. »
Orson Welles, *The Orson Welles Story*

"Orson's lifelong attraction to the art that has as its very essence the blurring of the line between reality and illusion was another piece of this same puzzle: Nothing gave him as much consistent pleasure as teasing audiences, and himself, with the many masks of magic."
Henry Jaglom

„Dass sich Orson ein Leben lang zu der Kunstform hingezogen fühlte, die im Grunde ihres Wesens die Trennungslinie zwischen Wirklichkeit und Illusion verwischt, war ein weiteres Stück des gleichen Puzzles: Nichts gab ihm auf Dauer so viel Freude, wie das Publikum – und sich selbst – mit den vielen Masken der Zauberei zu foppen."
Henry Jaglom

« L'attirance qu'Orson a éprouvée toute sa vie pour l'art dont l'essence même est de brouiller la frontière entre la réalité et l'illusion est une autre pièce du même puzzle. Rien ne lui procurait un plaisir aussi constant que de titiller le public, ainsi que lui-même, avec les nombreux masques de la magie. »
Henry Jaglom

STILL FROM 'FOLLOW THE BOYS' (1944)
Marlene Dietrich and magician Welles perform for soldiers. / Marlene Dietrich und Zauberkünstler Welles treten vor Soldaten auf. / Marlene Dietrich et Orson Welles présentent un numéro de magie à des soldats.

"Orson Welles is a kind of giant with the look of a child, a tree filled with birds and shadow, a dog that has broken its chain and lies down in the flower beds, an active idler, a wise madman, an island surrounded by people, a pupil asleep in class, a strategist who pretends to be drunk when he wants to be left in peace."
Jean Cocteau

„Orson Welles ist eine Art Riese, der wie ein Kind aussieht; ein Baum voller Vögel und Schatten; ein Hund, der sich von seiner Kette losgerissen und in ein Blumenbeet gelegt hat; ein aktiver Müßiggänger; ein weiser Irrer; eine Insel in einem Meer von Menschen; ein Schüler, der im Unterricht einschläft; ein Stratege, der so tut, als sei er betrunken, wenn er nicht gestört werden will."
Jean Cocteau

« Orson Welles est une manière de géant au regard enfantin, un arbre bourré d'oiseaux et d'ombre, un chien qui a cassé sa chaîne et se couche dans les plates-bandes, un paresseux actif, un fou sage, une solitude entourée de monde, un étudiant qui dort en classe, un stratège qui fait semblant d'être ivre quand il veut qu'on lui foute la paix. »
Jean Cocteau

**STILL FROM 'TOMORROW IS FOREVER'
(1945)**
A heart-filled wartime performance, opposite Natalie Wood. / Eine Vorstellung mit viel Herz, mitten im Krieg, an der Seite von Natalie Wood. / Un rôle plein d'émotion interprété pendant la guerre avec la petite Natalie Wood.

STILL FROM 'THE STRANGER' (1946)

As a Nazi fugitive hiding out in a small American town. /
Als nationalsozialistischer Flüchtling, der sich in einer
amerikanischen Kleinstadt versteckt. / Welles en fugitif
nazi caché dans une petite ville américaine.

ON THE SET OF 'THE STRANGER' (1946)
Directing Edward G. Robinson as a Nazi hunter. / Hier
gibt er Edward G. Robinson, der einen Nazijäger spielt,
Regieanweisungen. / Welles dirige Edward G. Robinson
en chasseur de nazis.

STILL FROM 'THE STRANGER' (1946)
Reduced to hiding amongst literal gargoyles. / Dazu
erniedrigt, sich zwischen grotesken Figuren zu
verstecken. / Condamné à se cacher au milieu des
gargouilles.

STILL FROM 'THE STRANGER' (1946)
"Pure Dick Tracy," he laughed of this ghoulish cartoon
climax. / „Reiner Dick Tracy", kommentierte er lachend
diesen comichaften wie makabren Höhepunkt. / « Du
pur Dick Tracy », dira-t-il en riant de ce dénouement
digne d'une bande dessinée macabre.

"The people who've done well within the [Hollywood] system are the people whose instincts, whose desires [are in natural alignment with those of producers] - who want to make the kind of movie that producers want to produce. People who don't succeed - people who've had long, bad times; like [Jean] Renoir, for example, who I think was the best director, ever - are the people who didn't want to make the kind of pictures that producers want to make. Producers didn't want to make a Renoir picture, even if it was a success."
Orson Welles, 'The Orson Welles Story'

„Die Leute, die innerhalb des [Hollywood-]Systems erfolgreich waren, sind diejenigen, deren Instinkte und Wünsche [von Natur aus denen der Produzenten entsprechen] - die die Art von Film machen wollen, die Produzenten gerne produzieren. Leute ohne Erfolg - Leute, die lange Durststrecken hinter sich haben, wie zum Beispiel [Jean] Renoir, den ich für den besten Regisseur aller Zeiten halte -, das sind diejenigen, die nicht die Art von Film machen wollten, die Produzenten gerne produzieren. Produzenten wollten keine Renoir-Filme machen, selbst wenn sie erfolgreich waren."
Orson Welles, *The Orson Welles Story*

« Les gens qui réussissent au sein du système [hollywoodien] sont ceux dont les instincts, dont les désirs [s'accordent naturellement à ceux des producteurs], ceux qui veulent faire le genre de films que les producteurs souhaitent produire. Ceux qui ne réussissent pas, ceux qui ont connu de longues périodes difficiles - comme [Jean] Renoir, par exemple, que je considère comme le meilleur cinéaste de tous les temps -, sont ceux qui ne veulent pas faire le même genre de films que les producteurs. Les producteurs ne veulent pas faire un film de Renoir, même si c'est un succès. »
Orson Welles, *The Orson Welles Story*

ON THE SET OF 'THE STRANGER' (1946)
Welles worked hard within the Hollywood system, but their mutual needs were never met. / Welles arbeitete hart innerhalb des Hollywood-Systems, aber die beiden Seiten konnten ihre unterschiedlichen Interessen nie auf einen Nenner bringen. / Welles travaille dur au sein du système hollywoodien, mais ni l'un ni l'autre n'y trouvent leur compte.

STILL FROM 'BLACK MAGIC' (1947)
As Cagliostro, the legendary 18th-Century magician. /
Als Cagliostro, der legendäre Zauberkünstler aus dem
18. Jahrhundert. / Welles en Cagliostro, le célèbre
magicien du XVIIIᵉ siècle.

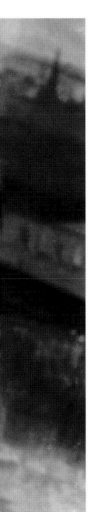

STILL FROM 'PRINCE OF FOXES' (1948)
Wicked, self-delighted as Cesare Borgia (Everett
Sloane, left). / Böse und selbstgefällig als Cesare Borgia
(Everett Sloane, links). / Welles, alias César Borgia,
se complaît dans la cruauté face à Everett Sloane.

ON THE SET OF 'THE LADY FROM SHANGHAI' (1948)
Errol Flynn (left) owned the yacht used in the film. / Die Jacht, die im Film verwendet wurde, gehörte Errol Flynn (links). / C'est à Errol Flynn (à gauche) qu'appartient le yacht utilisé dans le film.

ON THE SET OF 'THE LADY FROM SHANGHAI' (1948)
Boldly cutting away Rita Hayworth's famous flaming red locks. / Rita Hayworths berühmte feuerrote Locken fallen der Schere zum Opfer. / Orson Welles coupe sans états d'âme la célèbre chevelure rousse de Rita Hayworth.

"I'm aiming at you, lover. Killing you is like killing myself. But frankly, I'm tired of both of us."
Arthur Bannister aiming his pistol at Elsa, 'The Lady from Shanghai'

„*Ich ziele auf dich, meine Liebe. Dich zu töten ist wie mich selbst zu töten. Aber offen gesagt hab ich von uns beiden die Schnauze voll.*"
Arthur Bannister, während er mit seiner Pistole auf Elsa zielt, *Die Lady von Shanghai*

« *C'est toi que je vise, ma belle. Te tuer, c'est comme me tuer moi-même. Mais franchement, j'en ai marre de nous deux.* »
Arthur Bannister pointant son pistolet sur Elsa, *La Dame de Shanghaï*

ON THE SET OF 'THE LADY FROM SHANGHAI' (1948)
On location in a misty, atmospheric postwar San Francisco. / Bei Außendreharbeiten in einem nebligen, atmosphärischen San Francisco der Nachkriegszeit. / En extérieur dans l'atmosphère brumeuse du San Francisco d'après-guerre.

PAGES 74/75
STILL FROM 'THE LADY FROM SHANGHAI' (1948)
The wildly twisting plot fittingly climaxes in a hall of mirrors. / Die teuflisch verzwickte Handlung gipfelt passenderweise in einem Spiegelkabinett. / L'intrigue aux mille facettes se dénoue logiquement dans une galerie des glaces.

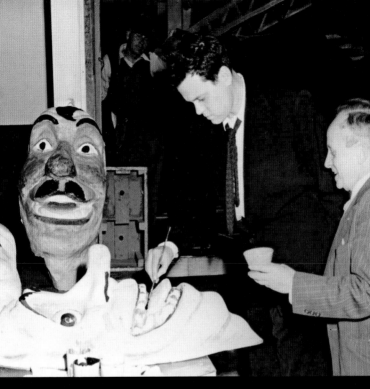

ON THE SET OF 'THE LADY FROM SHANGHAI' (1948)

Welles personally detailing the surrealist, playful, sinister funhouse climax. / Welles kümmert sich persönlich um die Details des surrealistischen, verspielten, düsteren Höhepunkts im Spiegelkabinett. / Welles retouche lui-même les masques grotesques de la scène surréaliste de la fête foraine.

STILL FROM 'MACBETH' (1948)
A Shakespeare epic, for the low-budget price of a western. / Ein Shakespeare-Epos mit dem schmalen Budget eines Westernfilms. / Une épopée shakespearienne pour le prix d'un modique western.

STILL FROM 'MACBETH' (1948)
The Weird Sisters, primitive and pagan. / Die Schicksalsschwestern, ursprünglich und heidnisch. / Les trois sorcières, païennes et primitives.

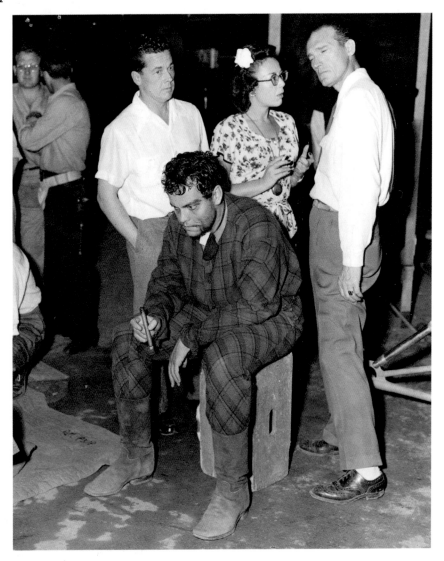

ON THE SET OF 'MACBETH' (1948)
Welles preparing himself for the psychologically
demanding central role. / Welles bereitet sich auf die
psychologisch anspruchsvolle Hauptrolle vor. / Welles
se prépare pour un rôle psychologiquement éprouvant.

STILL FROM 'MACBETH' (1948)
"Is this a dagger I see before me?" The murder of
Duncan. / „Ist das ein Dolch, was ich vor mir erblicke?" –
Die Ermordung Duncans. / « Est-ce une dague que je
vois devant moi ? » Le meurtre de Duncan.

ON THE SET OF 'MACBETH' (1948)
Another breather, another costume, another cigar. /
Noch eine Verschnaufpause, noch ein Kostüm, noch
eine Zigarre. / Changement de costume, le temps d'une
pause et d'un cigare.

PORTRAIT FROM 'MACBETH' (1948)
A false King, haunted by the spectre of his murdered
friend. / Ein falscher König wird vom Geist seines
ermordeten Freundes heimgesucht. / Un faux roi hanté
par le spectre de l'ami assassiné.

ON THE SET OF 'MACBETH' (1948)
These plaster cliffs also appear in countless cheap
westerns. / Diese Gipsklippen tauchen auch in
zahlreichen Billigwestern auf. / Ces falaises de plâtre
apparaissent également dans d'innombrables westerns
à deux sous.

ON THE SET OF 'MACBETH' (1948)
The three-week shoot created many anxious moments. / Die dreiwöchigen Dreharbeiten sorgten für zahlreiche Spannungen. / Les trois semaines de tournage sont ponctuées de nombreux moments de tension.

ON THE SET OF 'MACBETH' (1948)
During the battle sequences, Welles hid cameramen
(with costumes on backwards) to record the fighting
close-up. / Während der Schlachtszenen versteckte
Welles Kameraleute (die ihre Kostüme rückwärts
trugen), um die Kampfhandlungen in Nahaufnahme
filmen zu können. / Pendant les scènes de combats,
Welles cache les cameramen chargés de filmer les gros
plans en leur mettant un costume à l'envers.

*"I've spent too much energy on things that have
nothing to do with making a movie... It's [been]
about 2 percent movie-making and 98 percent
hustling. That's no way to spend a life."*
Orson Welles, 'The Orson Welles Story'

STILL FROM 'MACBETH' (1948)
Fully restored in 1985, this film is now fully appreciated (at last). / Der 1985 vollständig restaurierte Film findet nun (endlich) die verdiente Würdigung. / Entièrement restauré en 1985, ce film est enfin apprécié à sa juste valeur.

„Ich habe zu viel Energie mit Dingen verschwendet, die nichts mit Filmemachen zu tun haben ... Es war rund zwei Prozent Filmemachen und 98 Prozent Betteln. So kann man doch nicht sein Leben verbringen."
Orson Welles, *The Orson Welles Story*

« J'ai consacré trop d'énergie à des choses qui n'ont rien à voir avec le cinéma... Environ 2 pour cent pour la création et 98 pour cent pour faire le tapin. Ce n'est pas une vie. »
Orson Welles, *The Orson Welles Story*

ON THE SET OF 'THE THIRD MAN' (1949)
A gratuity from career-heaven, directed by Carol Reed
(right). / Eine gute Gabe aus dem Karrierehimmel,
inszeniert von Carol Reed (rechts). / Orson Welles au
sommet de sa carrière, dirigé par Carol Reed (à droite).

STILL FROM 'THE THIRD MAN' (1949)
A devilish, merry archetype – Harry Lime. / Ein
teuflischer, fröhlicher Archetyp: Harry Lime. / Harry
Lime, archétype joyeusement diabolique.

ON THE SET OF 'THE THIRD MAN' (1949)
Welles, Reed (right) and Joseph Cotten (seated, left)
have tea before recording one of the most famous
speeches in cinema history. / Welles, Reed (rechts) und
Joseph Cotten (sitzend, links) trinken zusammen Tee,
bevor sie einen der berühmtesten Monologe der
Filmgeschichte drehen. / Welles, Reed (à droite) et
Joseph Cotten (assis, à gauche) prennent le thé avant
de tourner l'une des tirades les plus célèbres de
l'histoire du cinéma.

*"In Italy for thirty years under the Borgias they
had warfare, terror, murder, bloodshed – they
produced Michelangelo, Leonardo da Vinci and
the Renaissance. In Switzerland they had brotherly
love, five hundred years of democracy and peace,
and what did that produce? The cuckoo clock."*
Harry Lime, 'The Third Man'

STILL FROM 'THE THIRD MAN' (1949)
High above the world, Harry shows Holly his chilling
perspective. / Hoch über dem Rest der Welt erläutert
Harry Holly seine erschreckende Weltanschauung. / Du
haut de la Grande Roue, Harry montre à Holly son
effrayante vision du monde.

„Unter den Borgias gab es in Italien dreißig
Jahre lang Krieg, Terror, Mord, Blutvergießen – sie
haben Michelangelo, Leonardo da Vinci und die
Renaissance hervorgebracht. In der Schweiz gab es
Nächstenliebe, fünfhundert Jahre Demokratie und
Frieden, und was ist dabei herausgekommen?
Die Kuckucksuhr!"
Harry Lime, *Der dritte Mann*

« En Italie, sous les Borgia, il y a eu trente ans de
guerre, de terreur, de meurtres et de carnages et
ils ont produit Michel-Ange, Léonard de Vinci et la
Renaissance. En Suisse, il y a eu l'amour fraternel,
cinq cents ans de paix et de démocratie, et qu'est-
ce que ça a produit ? Le coucou. »
Harry Lime, *Le Troisième Homme*

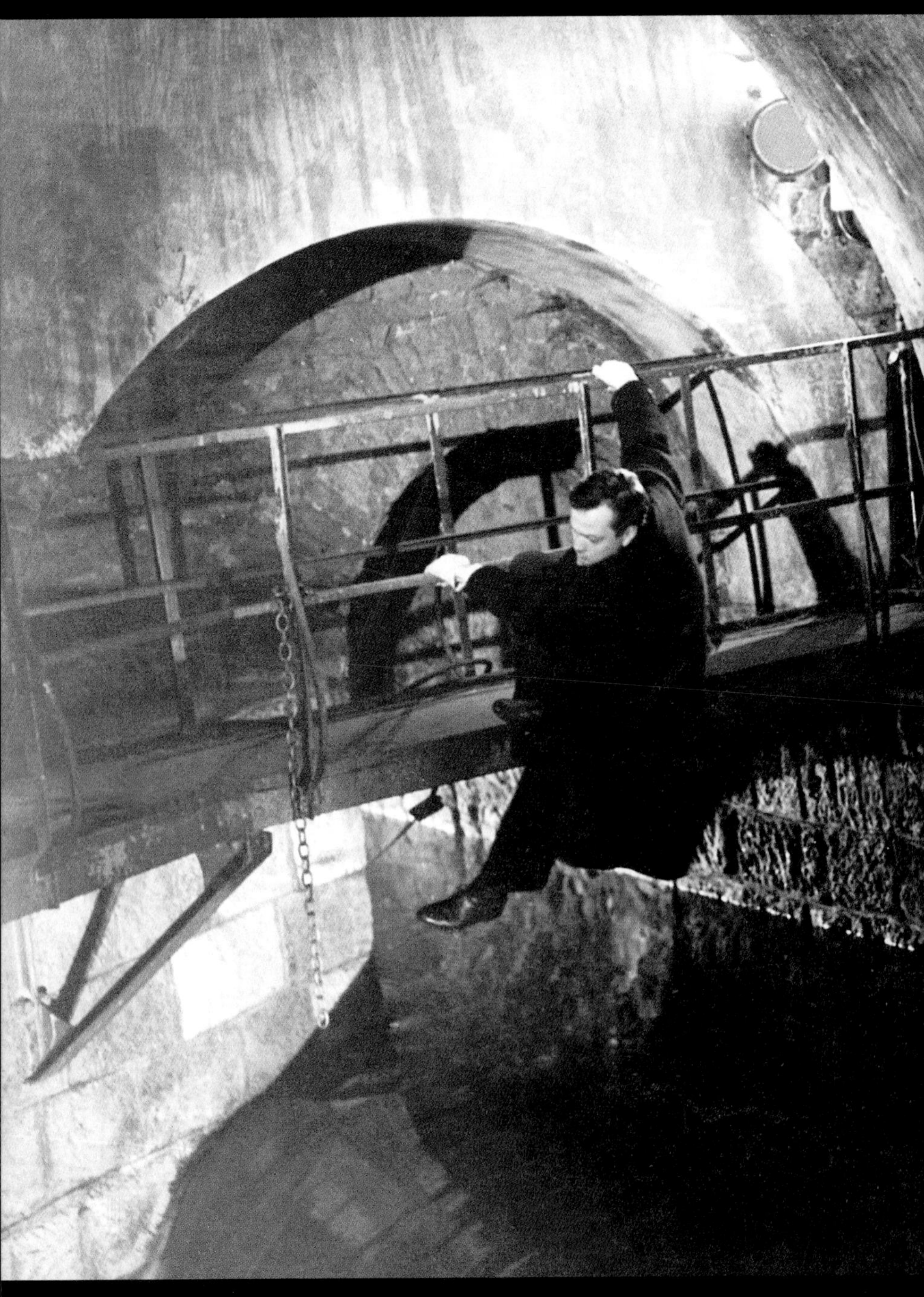

STILL FROM 'THE THIRD MAN' (1949)
Harry Lime, trapped – appropriately – like a rat, where
rats live. / Dort, wo die Ratten zu Hause sind, sitzt Harry
Lime – passenderweise – wie eine Ratte in der Falle. /
Harry Lime, fait comme un rat dans les immondices.

STILL FROM 'THE THIRD MAN' (1949)
Elegant archways, terrible stench: filming in actual
Vienna sewers. / Elegante Bogengänge, fürchterlicher
Gestank: Dreharbeiten in echten Wiener Kloaken. /
D'élégantes voûtes dans une abominable puanteur :
tournage dans les égouts de Vienne.

STILL FROM 'THE BLACK ROSE' (1950)
Cast Welles as an Asian warlord, and he was game. /
Auch die Rolle eines asiatischen Kriegsherrn nahm
Welles dankend an. / Orson Welles très à l'aise en
seigneur de guerre oriental.

ON THE SET OF 'THE BLACK ROSE' (1950)
"A King Player" is how Jeanne Moreau characterized
Welles as an actor. / Als „Königsmimen" beschrieb
Jeanne Moreau den Schauspieler Orson Welles. / Pour
Jeanne Moreau, Orson Welles est « un acteur roi ».

ON THE SET OF 'OTHELLO' (1952)
Suzanne Cloutier as Desdemona, exalted by Welles. /
Suzanne Cloutier als Desdemona, von Welles
gepriesen. / Suzanne Cloutier en Desdémone, glori-
fiée par Welles.

STILL FROM 'OTHELLO' (1952)
Surveying Moorish battlements with Micheál
MacLiammóir. / Mit Micheál MacLiammóir schaut
er sich maurische Zinnen an. / Sur les remparts
mauresques avec Micheál MacLiammóir.

"[T]hrough the turbulent vapors of his temperament there flows a broad river full of stars."
Micheál MacLiammóir, 'All For Hecuba'

„[D]urch die ungestümen Dünste seines Temperaments fließt ein breiter Strom voller Sterne."
Micheál MacLiammóir, *All For Hecuba*

« [À] travers les turbulentes vapeurs de son tempérament coule une large rivière pleine d'étoiles. »
Micheál MacLiammóir, *All For Hecuba*

STILL FROM 'OTHELLO' (1952)
Making spectacular use of existing architecture. / Auf spektakuläre Weise integriert er die vorhandene Architektur. / Utilisation spectaculaire de l'architecture existante.

STILL FROM 'OTHELLO' (1952)
With dead Desdemona: "I loved not wisely, but too well." / Mit der toten Desdemona: „ ... der nicht weislich liebte, aber zu sehr." / Près du corps de Desdémone : « J'ai aimé non pas sagement, mais trop bien. »

STILL FROM 'OTHELLO' (1952)
A final, candlelit glimpse of Welles as a romantic lead actor. / Ein letzter Blick im Kerzenschein auf Welles als romantischer Frauentyp. / Dernier aperçu d'Orson Welles en héros romantique à la lueur de la bougie.

CAMEOS

GASTROLLEN

RÔLES SECONDAIRES

PAGE 104
PORTRAIT FROM 'THE VIP'S' (1963)

STILL FROM 'TRENT'S LAST CASE' (1953)
Sigsbee Manderson (Welles) contemplates suicide in
this adaptation of E.C. Bentley's classic mystery. /
In dieser Verfilmung von E. C. Bentleys Krimiklassiker
spielt Sigsbee Manderson (Welles) mit dem Gedanken,
sich umzubringen. / Sigsbee Manderson (Welles) songe
au suicide dans cette adaptation du célèbre roman
d'E. C. Bentley.

**STILL FROM 'THREE CASES OF MURDER'
(1955)**
Welles, as Mountdrago, in another British mystery, this
time based on a story by W. Somerset Maugham. /
Welles als Mountdrago in einem weiteren britischen
Krimi, diesmal nach einer Geschichte von W. Somerset
Maugham. / Welles, alias Mountdrago, dans une autre
énigme britannique, tirée cette fois d'une nouvelle de
W. Somerset Maugham.

"Orson revealed his surprising capacity for collaboration. For all the mass of his own ego, he was able to apprehend other people's weakness and strength and to make creative use of them: he had a shrewd instinctive sense of when to bully or charm, when to be kind or savage... "
John Houseman, 'Run-Through'

„Orson ließ eine überraschende Fähigkeit zur Zusammenarbeit erkennen. Trotz der Masse seines eigenen Egos war er doch in der Lage, die Schwächen und Stärken anderer Menschen wahrzunehmen und sie schöpferisch zu nutzen: Er besaß einen scharfsinnigen Instinkt, der ihm sagte, wann er bedrohen und wann er betören musste, wann er charmant zu sein hatte und wann böse ..."
John Houseman, Run-Through

« Orson révéla son étonnante capacité de collaboration. Malgré l'ampleur de son propre ego, il était capable d'appréhender les forces et les faiblesses des autres et d'en faire un usage créatif. Il savait instinctivement quand les brutaliser ou les charmer, quand être doux ou sauvage... »
John Houseman, Run-Through

ON THE SET OF 'MR ARKADIN' (1955)

Welles melded two Harry Lime radio shows into one pulpish story and then filmed it guerrilla-style as usual. Here he is filming with co-star Robert Arden in Cannes. / Welles verschmolz zwei Harry-Lime-Hörspiele zu einer groschenromanhaften Geschichte und verfilmte sie dann wie üblich im Partisanenstil. Hier dreht er gerade mit Kollege Robert Arden in Cannes. / Welles fond trois épisodes des aventures radiophoniques de Harry Lime en une solide histoire qu'il filme comme toujours avec les moyens du bord. Il tourne ici à Cannes avec son partenaire Robert Arden.

STILL FROM 'MR ARKADIN' (1955)
A lethal battle of wills between Arkadin (Welles), an
enigmatic arms billionaire ... / Ein tödliches Messen der
Willenskräfte zwischen Gregory Arkadin (Welles),
einem rätselhaften Waffenmilliardär ... / Un terrible
bras de fer entre Arkadin (Welles), un mystérieux
milliardaire ...

STILL FROM 'MR ARKADIN' (1955)
... And Guy Van Stratten (Robert Arden), an American
hustler in love with the big man's daughter. /
... und Guy Van Stratten (Robert Arden), einem
amerikanischen Gauner, der sich in dessen Tochter
verliebt hat. /
... et Guy Van Stratten (Robert Arden), un jeune
maître chanteur amoureux de sa fille.

STILL FROM 'MR ARKADIN' (1955)
Paola Mori (aka Mrs Orson Welles) played the daughter
Raina Arkadin. Some have written that Welles created
this film for her, like Kane built an opera house for his
wife. / Paola Mori (alias Frau Orson Welles) spielte
Raina Arkadin, die Tochter. Einige Kritiker meinten,
Welles habe diesen Film eigens für sie geschrieben, so
wie Kane seiner Frau ein Opernhaus baute. / Paola Mori
(alias Mme Welles) interprète la fille d'Arkadin. Certains
pensent que Welles a créé ce film pour elle, comme
Kane a construit un opéra pour sa femme.

STILL FROM 'MR ARKADIN' (1955)
Arkadin's Spanish castle echoes Kane's Xanadu. /
Arkadins spanisches Schloss erinnert an Kanes
Xanadu. / Le château d'Arkadin en Espagne évoque
Xanadu, le palais de *Citizen Kane*.

STILL FROM 'MR ARKADIN' (1955)
Van Stratten's hunt for Arkadin's past associates is an
opportunity for some delightful cameos. Here is
Michael Redgrave as Burgomil Trebitsch. / Van Strattens
Jagd nach Arkadins einstigem Komplizen bietet die
Gelegenheit für einige köstliche Cameo-Auftritte. Hier
sieht man Michael Redgrave als Burgomil Trebitsch. /
La recherche des anciens complices d'Arkadin donne
lieu à de délicieuses apparitions, comme celle de
Michael Redgrave dans le rôle de Burgomil Trebitsch.

STILL FROM 'MR ARKADIN' (1955)
Akim Tamiroff, a Welles favorite, played Jacob Zouk. /
Akim Tamiroff, einer von Welles' Lieblingsschauspielern,
spielte Jacob Zouk. / Akim Tamiroff, l'un des acteurs
fétiches de Welles, interprète Jacob Zouk.

ON THE SET OF 'MOBY DICK' (1956)
Director John Huston and Welles became great friends. / Regisseur John Huston und Welles wurden dicke Freunde. / Welles et le réalisateur John Huston sont devenus de grands amis.

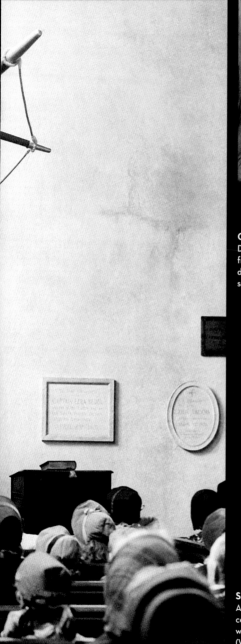

STILL FROM 'MOBY DICK' (1956)
A whale-obsessed sermon from Father Mapple (Welles, center). / Pastor Mapple (Welles, Mitte) hält eine walbesessene Predigt. / Sermon du père Mapple (Welles, au centre), obsédé par les baleines.

**PORTRAIT FROM 'THE LONG HOT SUMMER'
(1957)**
Co-starring with Paul Newman, in a story from William
Faulkner. / Mit Paul Newman in einer Geschichte von
William Faulkner. / Aux côtés de Paul Newman dans une
histoire tirée de William Faulkner.

STILL FROM 'THE ROOTS OF HEAVEN' (1958)
Once again, directed by John Huston – adapting Romain
Gary. / Wieder einmal unter der Regie John Hustons –
in einer Romain-Gary-Verfilmung. / Une fois encore
dans un film de John Huston adapté de Romain Gary.

1851-25

STILL FROM 'TOUCH OF EVIL' (1958)
Hank Quinlan (Welles) is a corrupt lawman opposed by
Ramón Vargas (Charlton Heston). / Der korrupte
Gesetzeshüter Hank Quinlan (Welles) ist der
Gegenspieler von Ramón Vargas (Charlton Heston). /
Hank Quinlan (Welles) est un policier corrompu auquel
s'oppose Ramón Vargas (Charlton Heston).

ON THE SET OF 'TOUCH OF EVIL' (1958)
A film and a role which have deepened in popularity
over time. / Ein Film und eine Rolle, die im Laufe der
Jahre immer mehr Freunde fanden. / Un film et un rôle

STILL FROM 'TOUCH OF EVIL' (1958)
Janet Leigh (center), menaced as ever by psychos in
a motel. / Janet Leigh (Mitte) wird wieder einmal von
Psychopathen in einem Motel bedroht. / Janet Leigh
(au centre), comme toujours menacée par des
psychopathes dans un sinistre motel.

STILL FROM 'TOUCH OF EVIL' (1958)
Framing an unconscious victim for the murder of an
unwitting one. / Einem bewusstlosen Opfer wird ein
unbeabsichtigter Mord angehängt. / Welles fait porter
le chapeau d'un meurtre involontaire à un malheureux
innocent.

"I think I made, essentially, a mistake, staying in movies. But it's a mistake I can't regret, because it's like saying, 'I shouldn't have stayed married to that woman, but I did because I love her. I would've been more successful if I hadn't been married to her...' You know?"
Orson Welles, 'The Orson Welles Story'

„Ich glaube, ich habe im Grunde einen Fehler gemacht, als ich beim Film blieb. Aber ich kann diesen Fehler nicht bedauern, weil es so wäre, als sagte man: ‚Ich hätte nicht mit dieser Frau verheiratet bleiben sollen, aber ich blieb es, weil ich sie liebe. Ich hätte mehr Erfolg gehabt, wenn ich nicht mit ihr verheiratet gewesen wäre ...' – Verstehen Sie?"
Orson Welles, *The Orson Welles Story*

« Je crois que j'ai fondamentalement fait une erreur en restant dans le cinéma. Mais c'est une erreur que je ne peux regretter, car c'est comme dire "Je n'aurais pas dû rester avec cette femme, mais je l'ai fait parce que je l'aimais. J'aurais mieux réussi si je n'avais pas été marié avec elle..." Vous comprenez ? »
Orson Welles, *The Orson Welles Story*

STILL FROM 'COMPULSION' (1959)
Cross-examining Adolphe Menjou (right) in a superb performance. / Das Kreuzverhör von Adolphe Menjou (rechts) war eine hervorragende Leistung. / Interrogatoire d'Adolphe Menjou (à droite) dans un superbe numéro d'acteur.

STILL FROM 'FERRY TO HONG KONG' (1959)
Captain Hart is a role of which Welles was long fond. /
Kapitän Hart war eine Rolle, an die sich Welles noch
lange Zeit gerne erinnerte. / Le capitaine Hart est un
rôle auquel Welles sera longtemps attaché.

STILL FROM 'FERRY TO HONG KONG' (1959)
Welles admired comic W.C. Fields – and it shows here. /
Welles bewunderte den Komiker W. C. Fields – wie man
hier sieht. / Comme il le prouve ici, Welles admire l'acteur comique W. C. Fields.

STILL FROM 'FERRY TO HONG KONG' (1959)
Curt Jurgens (right) as a man haplessly trapped on this ferry. / Curd Jürgens (rechts) spielt einen Mann, der unglücklich auf dieser Fähre in der Falle sitzt. / Curt Jurgens (à droite) en homme irrémédiablement prisonnier de l'embarcation.

STILL FROM 'FERRY TO HONG KONG' (1959)
Even at his most comic, there are layers of authentic despair. / Selbst in seinen komischsten Momenten entdeckt man Schichten echter Verzweiflung. / Même ses scènes les plus comiques contiennent un véritable désespoir.

STILL FROM 'CRACK IN THE MIRROR' (1960)
A melodramatic love triangle, directed by Richard
Fleischer. / Eine melodramatische Dreierbeziehung,
inszeniert von Richard Fleischer. / Un triangle amoureux
mélodramatique réalisé par Richard Fleischer.

STILL FROM 'THE TARTARS' (1961)
As a Mongol chief bent on conquering Russia, circa
900 AD. / Als Mongolenherrscher, der um 900 n. Chr.
unbedingt Russland erobern will. / En chef mongol
décidé à conquérir la Russie vers l'an 900.

'One should make movies innocently – the way Adam and Eve named the animals, their first day in the garden. ... Learn from your own interior vision of things, as if there had never been a D.W. Griffith, or a [Sergei] Eisenstein, or a [John] Ford, or a [Jean] Renoir, or anybody."
Orson Welles, 'The Orson Welles Story'

„Man sollte Filme auf unschuldige Weise machen – so wie Adam und Eva den Tieren Namen gaben, am ersten Tag im Paradies. ... Du musst von deiner eigenen inneren Vorstellung der Dinge lernen, als ob es nie einen D. W. Griffith oder einen [Sergej] Eisenstein oder einen [John] Ford oder einen [Jean] Renoir oder sonst jemanden gegeben hätte."
Orson Welles, *The Orson Welles Story*

« On devrait faire des films innocemment, comme Adam et Ève lorsqu'ils nommèrent les animaux le premier jour dans le jardin d'Éden. [...] Apprendre de sa propre vision intérieure des choses, comme si D. W. Griffith, [Serge] Eisenstein, [John] Ford ou [Jean] Renoir n'avaient jamais existé. »
Orson Welles, *The Orson Welles Story*

STILL FROM 'THE TRIAL' (1962)
Anthony Perkins, as Franz Kafka's dreamy sufferer, Josef K. / Anthony Perkins als Franz Kafkas leidgeplagter Träumer Josef K. / Anthony Perkins dans le rôle de Josef K., le malheureux héros de Franz Kafka.

PAGES 134 & 135
STILLS FROM 'THE TRIAL' (1962)
Filming in Yugoslavia, using Soviet era buildings (left) and sets of Welles' own design (right). / Bei den Dreharbeiten im ehemaligen Jugoslawien verwendete Welles sowohl Gebäude aus der Zeit der kommunistischen Diktatur (links) als auch Bühnenbilder nach eigenen Entwürfen (rechts). / Tournage en Yougoslavie, dans des immeubles de l'ère soviétique (à gauche) et des décors conçus par Welles (à droite).

STILL FROM 'THE TRIAL' (1962)
Josef K. is not a victim, but a self-serving, sneering individual afraid that the system will find him out. / Josef K. ist kein Opfer, sondern eine eigennützige, hochnäsige Person, die Angst davor hat, das System könne ihr auf die Schliche kommen. / Josef K. n'est pas une victime, mais un individu égoïste et sournois qui craint d'être démasqué par le système.

PAGE 138
STILL FROM 'THE TRIAL' (1962)
Leni (Romy Schneider), the Advocate's sexy nurse, is aroused by accused men. / Leni (Romy Schneider), die erotische Krankenschwester des Rechtsanwalts, fühlt sich von Beschuldigten sexuell angezogen. / Leni (Romy Schneider), la séduisante infirmière de l'avocat, est attirée par les hommes inculpés.

PAGE 139
STILL FROM 'THE TRIAL' (1962)
Leni reveals all the lurid details of her liaisons to the Advocate (Welles). / Leni enthüllt dem Rechtsanwalt (Welles) all die schmutzigen Einzelheiten ihrer Liebesaffären. / Leni révèle les détails les plus scabreux de ses liaisons à l'avocat (Welles).

CANNES FILM FESTIVAL (1954)
Welles relaxing with fellow filmmakers Mack Sennett and Anatole Litvak. / Welles entspannt sich mit seinen Regiekollegen Mack Sennett und Anatole Litvak. / Moment de détente avec les réalisateurs Mack Sennett et Anatole Litvak.

ON THE SET OF 'ROGOPAG' (1963)
Taking direction from Pier Paolo Pasolini. / Hier nimmt er Regieanweisungen von Pier Paolo Pasolini entgegen. / Sous la direction de Pier Paolo Pasolini.

LOVING LIFE

LIEBESLEBEN

AMOURS ET PASSIONS

ON THE SET OF 'CHIMES AT MIDNIGHT' (1966)
Dressing his daughter Beatrice, as Falstaff's angelic page. / Welles kleidet seine Tochter Beatrice an, die hier Falstaffs engelhaften Pagen mimt. / Welles habille sa fille Beatrice en angélique petit page.

STILL FROM 'CHIMES AT MIDNIGHT' (1966)
An intimate moment with Doll Tearsheet (Jeanne Moreau). / Ein Augenblick trauter Zweisamkeit mit Doll Tearsheet (Jeanne Moreau). / Moment d'intimité avec Doll Tearsheet (Jeanne Moreau).

PAGE 142
STILL FROM 'CHIMES AT MIDNIGHT' (1966)
Sir John Falstaff (Welles) is one of Shakespeare's greatest creations. / Sir John Falstaff (Welles) ist eine der genialsten Gestalten Shakespeares. / Le personnage de Falstaff (Welles) est l'une des plus grandes créations de Shakespeare.

"Those of us who were close to Orson had long been aware of the obsessive part his father used to play in his life. Much of what he had accomplished so precociously had been done out of a furious need to prove himself in the eyes of a man who was no longer there to see it. Now that success had come, in quantities and of a kind that his father had never dreamed of, this conflict, far from being assuaged, seemed to grow more intense and consuming."
John Houseman, 'Run-Through'

„Diejenigen von uns, die Orson nahestanden, wussten seit langem, welch obsessive Rolle sein Vater in seinem Leben zu spielen pflegte. Viele seiner frühreifen Leistungen erbrachte er aus dem dringenden Bedürfnis, sich in den Augen eines Mannes zu beweisen, der nicht mehr da war, es zu sehen. Nun, da sich der Erfolg eingestellt hatte - in einem Maße und auf eine Art, die sich sein Vater nie erträumt hätte -, schien sich dieser Konflikt nicht nur nicht beizulegen, sondern, im Gegenteil, noch intensiver und kräfteverzehrender zu werden."
John Houseman, *Run-Through*

« Ceux d'entre nous qui étaient proches d'Orson étaient depuis longtemps conscients du rôle obsessionnel que son père avait joué dans sa vie. Beaucoup de ce qu'il avait accompli si précocement découlait d'un furieux besoin de prouver de quoi il était capable aux yeux d'un homme qui n'était plus là pour le voir. Maintenant qu'il avait atteint un succès dont son père n'aurait jamais pu imaginer la nature ni l'ampleur, ce conflit, loin d'être apaisé, semblait devenir plus intense et plus dévorant. »
John Houseman, *Run-Through*

STILL FROM 'CHIMES AT MIDNIGHT' (1966)
Keith Baxter (left), superb as Prince Hal, the future Henry V. / Keith Baxter (links), hervorragend als Prinz Hal, der künftige Heinrich V. / Keith Baxter (à gauche), superbe dans le rôle du prince Hal, le futur Henry V.

18

STILL FROM 'CHIMES AT MIDNIGHT' (1966)
Heavily armoured knights, comically lowered onto their
steeds. / Ritter in schweren Rüstungen werden auf
ulkige Weise auf ihre Pferde gesetzt. / Chevaliers vêtus
de lourdes armures hissés sur leurs montures telles des
marionnettes.

PAGES 150/151
**ON THE SET OF 'CHIMES AT MIDNIGHT'
(1966)**
Platforms allow dynamic visuals, and erase modern
cityscapes. / Plattformen ermöglichen eine dynamische
Bildgestaltung und lassen moderne Stadtlandschaften
verschwinden. / L'utilisation de plates-formes dynamise
les visuels tout en gommant les immeubles modernes.

STILL FROM 'CHIMES AT MIDNIGHT' (1966)
Iconic good-heartedness. "Banish Falstaff, and banish all
the world." / Symbolische Gutherzigkeit. „Verbannt Ihr
Falstaff, verbannt Ihr die ganze Welt." / La bonté faite
homme. « Bannissez Falstaff, vous bannirez le monde
entier. »

STILL FROM 'CHIMES AT MIDNIGHT' (1966)
Henry IV (John Gielgud, left), scolds his "unthrifty
son." / Heinrich IV. (John Gielgud, links) schilt seinen
„verschwenderischen Sohn". / Henry IV (John Gielgud,
à gauche), gourmande son « fils peu économe ».

STILL FROM 'CHIMES AT MIDNIGHT' (1966)
Cast out by his former friend, the new king. /
Von seinem ehemaligen Freund, dem neuen König,
verstoßen. / Chassé par son ancien ami, le nouveau roi.

STILL FROM 'IS PARIS BURNING?' (1966)
As Consul Raoul Nordling, amid the flight of the Nazis
from Paris. / Als Konsul Raoul Nordling zwischen den
aus Paris flüchtenden Nationalsozialisten. / En consul
Raoul Nordling, lors de la fuite des nazis de Paris.

STILL FROM 'CASINO ROYALE' (1967)
Opposite Peter Sellers, spoofing James Bond. / Neben
Peter Sellers in einer James-Bond-Parodie. / Face à
Peter Sellers dans une parodie de James Bond.

PAGES 156/157
**ON THE SET OF 'A MAN FOR ALL SEASONS'
(1966)**
Lighting up between takes with director Fred
Zinnemann. / Raucherpause beim Dreh mit Regisseur
Fred Zinnemann. / Pause cigare entre deux prises avec
le metteur en scène Fred Zinnemann.

ON THE SET OF 'THE SAILOR FROM GIBRALTAR' (1967)

Friendship with Jeanne Moreau was a great mainstay of his life. / Die Freundschaft zu Jeanne Moreau war eine der Hauptstützen seines Lebens. / Son amitié avec Jeanne Moreau est l'un des piliers de son existence.

"To me, Orson is so much like a destitute king. A 'destitute' king, not because he was thrown away from the kingdom, but [because] on this earth, the way the world is, there is no kingdom good enough for Orson Welles."
Jeanne Moreau

STILL FROM 'I'LL NEVER FORGET WHAT'S 'ISNAME' (1967)
A fictional scene, but one he enacted in reality, on a daily basis. / Eine erfundene Szene, die er jedoch in der Wirklichkeit tagtäglich durchlebte. / Scène de fiction qu'il accomplit chaque jour dans la vraie vie.

„Für mich ist Orson wie ein verarmter König. ‚Verarmt' nicht deshalb, weil er aus seinem Königreich hinausgeworfen wurde, sondern [weil] auf dieser Erde, so wie die Welt nun einmal ist, kein Königreich gut genug ist für Orson Welles."
Jeanne Moreau

« Pour moi, Orson est comme un roi destitué. "Destitué" non pas parce qu'il a été chassé du royaume, mais [parce que] sur cette terre, dans le monde tel qu'il est, il n'existe pas de royaume assez bien pour Orson Welles. »
Jeanne Moreau

ON THE SET OF 'OEDIPUS THE KING' (1968)
A study in concentration. / Vorbildliche Konzentration. /
Un modèle de concentration.

STILL FROM 'HOUSE OF CARDS' (1968)
As a fascist hoping to overthrow the French
government. / Als Faschist hofft er, die französische
Regierung zu stürzen. / En fasciste espérant renverser
le gouvernement français.

STILL FROM 'THE IMMORTAL STORY' (1968)
Mr Clay (Welles) purchases Virginie's consent to turn
a fable into a reality. / Mr. Clay (Welles) erkauft sich
Virginies Zustimmung, eine erfundene Geschichte
wahr werden zu lassen. / Mr Clay (Welles) achète le
consentement de Virginie pour transformer une fable
en réalité.

STILL FROM 'THE IMMORTAL STORY' (1968)
Virginie Ducrot (Jeanne Moreau) is a fallen beauty
from a once great family. / Virginie Ducrot (Jeanne
Moreau) ist eine gefallene Schönheit aus einer einst
bedeutenden Familie. / Virginie Ducrot (Jeanne
Moreau) est une beauté déchue issue d'une ancienne
grande famille.

STILL FROM 'THE IMMORTAL STORY' (1968)
The impotent Clay wants to prove that he is powerful
by making others do his bidding. / Der impotente Clay
möchte seine Macht unter Beweis stellen, indem er
andere nach seiner Pfeife tanzen lässt. / Impuissant,
Clay tente d'affirmer son pouvoir en imposant sa
volonté à autrui.

STILL FROM 'THE IMMORTAL STORY' (1968)
Virginie and the sailor (Norman Eshley) enact the story
of the sailor who is paid to make love to a beautiful
woman. / Virginie und der Seemann (Norman Eshley)
spielen die Geschichte eines Matrosen, der für sein
Liebesspiel mit einer schönen Frau bezahlt wird. /
Virginie et le marin (Norman Eshley) accomplissent le
mythe du marin payé pour faire l'amour à une femme.

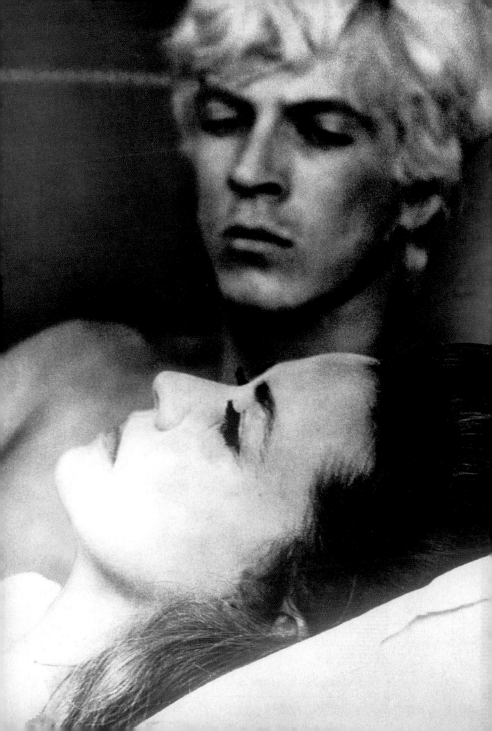

STILL FROM 'THE SOUTHERN STAR' (1969)
A game of draughts, played with drink, amid the African
diamond trade. / Ein Damespiel mit Drinks in der
afrikanischen Diamantenindustrie. / Jeu de dames bien
arrosé sur fond de commerce de diamants en Afrique.

STILL FROM 'CATCH-22' (1970)
General Dreedle (Welles) tries to pin a medal on a
naked Captain Yossarian (Alan Arkin): "This man is out
of uniform!" / General Dreedle (Welles) versucht, dem
nackten Captain Yossarian (Alan Arkin) einen Orden
anzuheften: „Der Mann hat ja keine Uniform an!" / Le
général Dreedle (Welles) tente d'épingler une médaille
sur la poitrine nue du capitaine Yossarian (Alan Arkin) :
« Il manque un uniforme à cet homme ! »

STILL FROM 'A SAFE PLACE' (1971)
With Tuesday Weld (left) for Henry Jaglom, a young
director friend. / Mit Tuesday Weld (links) für einen
befreundeten jungen Regisseur, Henry Jaglom. /
Tournage avec Tuesday Weld (à gauche) pour un ami, le
jeune réalisateur Henry Jaglom.

PAGES 170 & 171
STILLS FROM 'TEN DAYS' WONDER' (1971)
An interesting performance in a slightly plodding
mystery from a story by Ellery Queen, co-starring
Marlène Jobert (top right), and directed by Claude
Chabrol (bottom right). / Eine interessante
schauspielerische Leistung in einer etwas schleppenden
Krimiverfilmung nach Ellery Queen, mit Marlène Jobert
(oben rechts) unter der Regie von Claude Chabrol
(unten rechts). / Un numéro d'acteur intéressant dans
un thriller quelque peu poussif tiré d'un roman d'Ellery
Queen et réalisé par Claude Chabrol (en bas à droite),
avec Marlène Jobert (en haut à droite).

STILL FROM 'A SAFE PLACE' (1971)
At home (as ever) in the role of a magician. / Zu Hause
(wie immer) in der Rolle des Zauberkünstlers. / Très à
l'aise (comme toujours) dans ce rôle de magicien.

"[T]he man I got to know so well in no way resembled the mythical mask-wearer that everyone else saw and believed him to be. I discovered an incredibly open, deeply warm, and profoundly human friend, one who was generous to an unbelievable fault, was caring and concerned, and was vulnerable to the point of such fragility that he could be wounded terribly by the unaware, casual, critical statement of almost any outsider. I was always astounded by the way in which so many who did not know him viewed him as an arrogant, terrifying, egocentric ogre. They approached him with so much diffidence and fear as to set him up in such a way that his only possible response would be to satisfy their expectations. The Mask would win again."

Henry Jaglom

STILL FROM 'TREASURE ISLAND' (1972)
As Long John Silver. / Als Long John Silver. / Dans le rôle de Long John Silver.

PAGES 174 & 175
STILLS FROM 'F FOR FAKE' (1974)
Movie magic with a spiritual twin, artist Oja Kodar (bottom right). / Filmzauber mit einer Seelenverwandten, der Künstlerin Oja Kodar (unten rechts). / Magie cinématographique avec une âme sœur, l'artiste Oja Kodar (en bas à droite).

STILL FROM 'BUTTERFLY' (1981)
A working actor, opposite Pia Zadora. /
Ein Schauspieler bei der Arbeit, neben
Pia Zadora. / Un acteur au travail face à Pia Zadora.

„[D]er Mensch, den ich so gut kennen lernte, glich in
keiner Weise dem mythischen Maskenträger, den
alle anderen in ihm sahen und für den sie ihn hielten.
Ich entdeckte einen erstaunlich offenen,
warmherzigen und zutiefst menschlichen Freund, der
unglaublich großzügig, fürsorglich und besorgt
war und so empfindlich, dass er schrecklich verletzt
werden konnte durch eine unbedachte, zufällige
kritische Bemerkung irgendeines Außenstehenden.
Ich war immer verblüfft, wie ihn viele, die ihn nicht
kannten, als einen fürchterlichen, arroganten,
selbstsüchtigen Oger sahen. Sie traten mit solcher
Schüchternheit an ihn heran, dass seine einzig
mögliche Reaktion nur sein konnte, ihre Erwartungen
zu erfüllen. Die Maske hatte wieder gewonnen."
Henry Jaglom

ON THE SET OF 'THE OTHER SIDE OF THE WIND' (1970–76)

Directing John Huston (right), in a still-unreleased magnum opus. / In einem noch immer unveröffentlichten Meisterwerk gibt er Kollege John Huston (rechts) Regieanweisungen. / Welles dirige John Huston (à droite) dans une grande œuvre inachevée.

« [L]'homme que j'ai si bien connu ne ressemblait en rien au mythe du personnage masqué que tout le monde voyait en lui. J'ai découvert un ami incroyablement ouvert, extrêmement chaleureux et profondément humain, un être généreux à l'excès, bienveillant et attentif, et vulnérable au point de pouvoir être terriblement blessé par la critique inconsciente et désinvolte de n'importe quel étranger. J'étais toujours ébahi de la façon dont ceux qui ne le connaissaient pas le considéraient comme un ogre arrogant, terrifiant et égocentrique. Ils l'abordaient avec tant de timidité et de crainte que sa seule réaction possible était de satisfaire leurs attentes. Le Masque reprenait le dessus. »
Henry Jaglom

3
CHRONOLOGY

CHRONOLOGIE

CHRONOLOGIE

6 May 1915 George Orson Welles is born in Kenosha, Wisconsin.

9 May 1924 His mother Beatrice, to whom he was close, dies within days of his ninth birthday.

1925-1930 The Todd School. As a student at this innovative, trailblazing institute, young Orson plays Mary in the Christmas play and Jesus at the Easter play. Above all, he is permitted to act in or direct most of Shakespeare for paying audiences before he graduates aged 15.

1931-1933 Appears on the Dublin stage playing a variety of roles as middle-aged men, with convincing relish. Marries his first sweetheart, heiress Virginia Nicholson. Attracts the attention of playwright Thornton Wilder, who writes the letters of introduction that launch young Orson's prodigious early career in the New York Theater.

1934-1938 Teams with producer John Houseman and stages the so-called "Voodoo" *Macbeth*, a fascist era take on *Julius Caesar*, a politically and (as it turns out) stylistically radical musical, *The Cradle Will Rock* and *Faust*. When the pair adapt H.G. Wells' classic *War of the Worlds* on radio, over a million people panic throughout the United States, and Welles' name circles the globe. Franklin Roosevelt, who becomes personally fond of Welles, encourages him to consider a political career.

1939-1942 Welles and Houseman head to Hollywood, where RKO studios offer Welles a dream three-picture deal in which he will have complete control over casting and cutting. This breeds resentment throughout the filmmaking community. To this day, Welles is the only first-time director who was ever world famous before he stood on a film set. *Citizen Kane* (1941) causes firestorms of controversy with newspaper magnate William Randolph Hearst, who regards the film (not without reason) as a spoof on himself. Welles prevails in their battle – but becomes a ripe target for bad publicity as he heads to South America to make a wartime documentary. Personal and diplomatic disasters follow – among them the accidental death by drowning of his leading man, a peasant fisherman and folkloric hero in Brazil. The fallout capsizes Welles' career in Hollywood. His second film as director, *The Magnificent Ambersons* (1942), loses close to an hour of material on the cutting table. His dream-contract with RKO is nullified.

PORTRAIT OF THE ARTIST AS A YOUNG MAN
At age 12 or 13, but looking 16, at the Todd School. / Im Alter von 12 oder 13 Jahren an der Todd-Schule sah er bereits wie 16 aus. / À 12 ou 13 ans (il en paraît 16) à la Todd School.

1943–1956 Having divorced Virginia Nicholson in the late 1930s, Welles marries screen goddess Rita Hayworth in 1943. He stays afloat professionally by acting in films for other filmmakers, pursuing a career in radio as a commentator on politics. After the death of Franklin Roosevelt in 1945, few encourage him further. Instead he presses forward as a film director, working primarily in Europe after his marriage to Hayworth disintegrates. While in Italy in the early 1950s, he meets and marries Paola Mori, a countess he casts in *Mr Arkadin*. In 1956 they return to the U.S. with their daughter Beatrice. (She is the youngest of Welles' three children – including a daughter, Christopher, born in 1933, and Rebecca, 1944–2004.)

1957–1967 Welles gets a second lease on life as a filmmaker. *Citizen Kane*, long buried, is now widely considered a masterpiece. During this ten-year period, Welles makes two of his greatest films, *Touch of Evil* (1958) and *Chimes at Midnight* (1966), as well as an admirable adaptation of Kafka, *The Trial* (1962), and another of Isak Dinesen's *The Immortal Story* (1967).

1968–1985 Long years of hardship follow, in which only two films are completed – the cinematic essay *F for Fake* (1974) and an essay memoir, *Making Othello* (1978). Many others are begun, but fall afoul of money troubles (Welles had tax problems dating back to the mid-1940s) or critical meanness. Welles found himself either having to compete, in the minds of many, with his early successes, or to defend his early success against the revisionist attacks of such influential commentators as Pauline Kael. He nevertheless pressed on with his work, which he supported through bread and butter acting jobs.

9 October 1985 Welles dies at his typewriter, scripting a shot list for his next day's work – a film long in progress about magicians and magic acts – which he was to direct the next day on a soundstage at UCLA.

MARRIAGE OF ORSON WELLES AND RITA HAYWORTH (1943)
Joseph Cotten, best man and great friend. / Joseph Cotten, Trauzeuge und guter Freund. / Joseph Cotten, grand ami et témoin.

MAGIC ACT
He performed magic whenever and wherever he was
invited. / Wo immer und wann immer man ihn darum
bat, führte er Zaubertricks vor. / Welles exécute des
numéros de magie partout où on l'invite.

CHRONOLOGIE

6. Mai 1915 George Orson Welles wird in Kenosha, Wisconsin (USA), geboren.

9. Mai 1924 Seine Mutter Beatrice, der er sehr nahestand, stirbt wenige Tage nach seinem neunten Geburtstag.

1925–1930 Die Todd-Schule: Als Schüler an dieser bahnbrechend innovativen Institution spielt der junge Orson die Maria im Weihnachtskrippenspiel und den Jesus im Osterspiel. Vor allem aber gestattet man ihm, vor zahlendem Publikum in den meisten Shakespeare-Stücken mitzuspielen oder sie zu inszenieren, bevor er die Schule im Alter von 15 Jahren abschließt.

1931–1933 In Dublin steht er sichtlich vergnügt in diversen Rollen als Mann mittleren Alters auf der Bühne. Er heiratet seine erste Liebe, die Erbin Virginia Nicholson. Der Dramatiker Thornton Wilder wird auf ihn aufmerksam und schreibt für ihn Referenzbriefe, die den erstaunlichen Aufstieg des jungen Orsons in der New Yorker Theaterszene in die Wege leiten.

1934–1938 Er schließt sich mit dem Produzenten John Houseman zusammen und inszeniert den sogenannten „Voodoo" *Macbeth*, eine Interpretation von *Julius Caesar* im Zeitalter des Faschismus, das politisch und (wie sich herausstellt) stilistisch radikale Musical *The Cradle Will Rock* sowie *Faust*. Als die beiden den Science-Fiction-Klassiker *Der Krieg der Welten* von H. G. Wells als Hörspiel senden, geraten mehr als eine Million Amerikaner in Panik, und der Name Orson Welles geht um die Welt. Franklin D. Roosevelt, der persönliche Sympathien für Welles hegt, möchte ihn zu einer Karriere in der Politik überreden.

1939–1942 Welles und Houseman gehen nach Hollywood, wo die RKO-Studios Welles einen traumhaften Vertrag über drei Filme anbieten, bei denen er die vollständige Kontrolle über Besetzung und Schnitt erhält. Dadurch fällt er bei neidischen Kollegen in Ungnade. Bis heute ist Welles der einzige Filmregisseur, der bereits vor seinem ersten Film weltberühmt war. *Citizen Kane* (1941) löst heftige Auseinandersetzungen mit dem Zeitungsmagnaten William Randolph Hearst aus, der den Film (nicht ohne Grund) als Parodie auf seine Person betrachtet. Welles behält in der Schlacht die Oberhand, wird aber schon bald wieder zur Zielscheibe negativer Berichterstattung, als er nach Südamerika geht, um dort einen Dokumentarfilm über den Krieg zu drehen. Es folgen persönliche und diplomatische Katastrophen – darunter das Ertrinken seines Hauptdarstellers, eines brasilianischen Bauern und Fischers, der in seiner Heimat als Volksheld galt. Für

Welles und seine Hollywood-Karriere beginnt ein schneller Abstieg. Seine zweite Regiearbeit, *Der Glanz des Hauses Amberson* (1942), wird am Schneidetisch um fast eine Stunde gekürzt. Sein Traumvertrag mit RKO wird storniert.

1943–1956 Nach seiner Scheidung von Virginia Nicholson Ende der 1930er Jahre heiratet Welles 1943 die Leinwandgöttin Rita Hayworth. Beruflich hält er sich als Schauspieler unter fremder Regie über Wasser und kommentiert im Rundfunk das politische Zeitgeschehen. Nach Franklin D. Roosevelts Tod 1945 fehlt ihm der Ansporn zu Höherem. Stattdessen widmet er sich wieder seiner Karriere als Filmregisseur und arbeitet nach dem Scheitern seiner Ehe mit Hayworth hauptsächlich in Europa. Dabei lernt er Anfang der 1950er Jahre in Italien Paola Mori kennen, die in seinem Film *Herr Satan persönlich* eine Gräfin spielt, und heiratet sie. Im Jahre 1956 kehrt er mit seiner Frau und der gemeinsamen einjährigen Tochter Beatrice in die USA zurück. (Sie ist das jüngste seiner drei Kinder – die beiden anderen heißen Christopher [*1933] und Rebecca [1944–2004].)

1957–1967 Welles erhält eine zweite Chance als Filmemacher. *Citizen Kane*, lange Zeit unter Verschluss gehalten, gilt mittlerweile in weiten Kreisen als Meisterwerk. In diesem Jahrzehnt dreht Welles zwei seiner größten Filme, *Im Zeichen des Bösen* (1958) und *Falstaff* (1966), sowie die bemerkenswerte Kafka-Adaption *Der Prozeß* (1962) und eine Verfilmung von Isak Dinesens *Die unsterbliche Geschichte* unter dem Titel *Stunde der Wahrheit* (1967).

1968–1985 Es folgen wieder harte Zeiten, in denen er nur zwei Filme fertig stellt – den Filmessay *F wie Fälschung* (1974) und eine verfilmte Erinnerung, *Making Othello* (1978). Viele andere Projekte fängt er an, kann sie aber wegen gehässiger Kritiker oder akuten Geldmangels nie vollenden (Welles hatte bereits seit Mitte der vierziger Jahre Probleme mit dem Finanzamt). Einerseits messen ihn viele an seinen frühen Erfolgen, andererseits muss er diese immer wieder gegen revisionistische Angriffe einflussreicher Kommentatoren wie Pauline Kael verteidigen. Dennoch treibt er seine Arbeit voran, während er sich mit Schauspieljobs den Lebensunterhalt verdient.

9. Oktober 1985 Welles stirbt an seiner Schreibmaschine, als er die Liste der Einstellungen für den folgenden Tag tippt – für einen Film über Zauberer und ihre Kunststücke, der schon lange in Arbeit war und bei dem er am nächsten Tag in einer Studiohalle an der UCLA Regie führen sollte.

CHRONOLOGIE

6 mai 1915 Naissance de George Orson Welles à Kenosha, dans le Wisconsin.

9 mai 1924 Sa mère Beatrice, dont il est très proche, décède trois jours après son neuvième anniversaire.

1925-1930 Élève à la Todd School, un établissement pionnier, le jeune Orson joue le rôle de la Vierge Marie dans le spectacle de Noël et celui de Jésus à Pâques. Mais surtout, on lui permet de jouer ou de mettre en scène la plupart des pièces de Shakespeare pour un public payant avant même d'obtenir son diplôme à l'âge de 15 ans.

1931-1933 Se produit à Dublin dans divers rôles d'hommes mûrs qu'il interprète avec une délectation convaincante. Épouse sa première petite amie, l'héritière Virginia Nicholson. Attire l'attention du dramaturge Thornton Wilder, dont les lettres de recommandation lanceront ses prodigieux débuts au New York Theater.

1934-1938 Associé au producteur John Houseman, il monte le fameux *Macbeth* « vaudou », une version de *Jules César* transposée à l'époque fasciste, une comédie musicale politiquement et esthétiquement radicale intitulée *The Cradle Will Rock*, ainsi que *Faust*. Lorsque le tandem adapte *La Guerre des mondes* de H. G. Wells à la radio, l'émission fait souffler un vent de panique sur les États-Unis et le nom d'Orson Welles fait le tour de la planète. Franklin Roosevelt, qui se prend d'affection pour lui, tente de l'orienter vers la politique.

1939-1942 Welles et Houseman partent pour Hollywood, où la RKO offre au cinéaste un contrat de rêve pour trois films. Celui-ci lui garantit une totale liberté pour la distribution et le montage, ce qui attise la jalousie de ses confères. Welles reste à ce jour le seul cinéaste à avoir connu la célébrité internationale avant d'être monté sur un plateau de tournage. *Citizen Kane* (1941) suscite une vive controverse avec le magnat de la presse William Randolph Hearst, qui considère ce film (non sans raison) comme une satire de sa propre histoire. Si Welles remporte la bataille, il devient une proie facile pour ses détracteurs lorsqu'il se rend en Amérique du Sud pour y tourner un documentaire pendant la guerre. Il s'ensuit une série d'incidents personnels et diplomatiques, à commencer par la noyade accidentelle du personnage principal, un simple pêcheur considéré comme un héros populaire au Brésil. La mésaventure sonnera le glas de la carrière hollywoodienne d'Orson Welles. Son deuxième film, *La Splendeur des Amberson* (1942), est amputé de près

d'une heure au montage. Son contrat de rêve avec la RKO est invalidé.

1943-1956 Après avoir divorcé de Virginia Nicholson à la fin des années 1930, Welles épouse la star Rita Hayworth en 1943. Il maintient sa carrière à flot en jouant dans les films d'autres réalisateurs et en travaillant à la radio comme commentateur politique. Après la mort de Franklin Roosevelt en 1945, rares sont ceux qui l'encouragent à poursuivre dans cette voie. Il se lance donc à nouveau dans la mise en scène, travaillant principalement en Europe après sa rupture avec Rita Hayworth. En Italie, au début des années 1950, il rencontre et épouse Paola Mori, une comtesse à laquelle il confie un rôle dans *Dossier secret*. En 1956, ils rentrent aux États-Unis avec leur fille Beatrice. (C'est la plus jeune des trois filles d'Orson Welles, dont la première, Christopher, a vu le jour en 1933 et la deuxième, Rebecca - née en 1944 -, est décédée en 2004.)

1957-1967 Sa carrière de réalisateur prend un nouveau départ. *Citizen Kane*, longtemps enterré, est désormais considéré comme un chef-d'œuvre. Pendant cette décennie, Welles signe deux de ses meilleurs films, *La Soif du mal* (1958) et *Falstaff* (1966), ainsi que d'admirables adaptations du *Procès* de Kafka (1962) et d'*Une histoire immortelle* d'Isak Dinesen (1967).

1968-1985 Suivent de longues années de galère durant lesquelles il n'achève que deux films : *Vérité et mensonges* (1974), sorte d'essai sur l'art, et un récit de tournage, *Filming Othello* (1978). Beaucoup d'autres projets échoueront faute de moyens (les démêlés de Welles avec le fisc remontent au milieu des années 1940) ou sous les coups de la critique. Welles se retrouve contraint de se mesurer à ses premiers succès ou de les défendre contre les remises en cause de critiques aussi influents que Pauline Kael. Il continue pourtant contre vents et marées, finançant ses propres projets à l'aide de rôles alimentaires dans d'autres films.

9 octobre 1985 Welles succombe à une crise cardiaque devant sa machine à écrire, alors qu'il tape la liste des plans à tourner le lendemain pour un film depuis longtemps en cours, consacré à la magie.

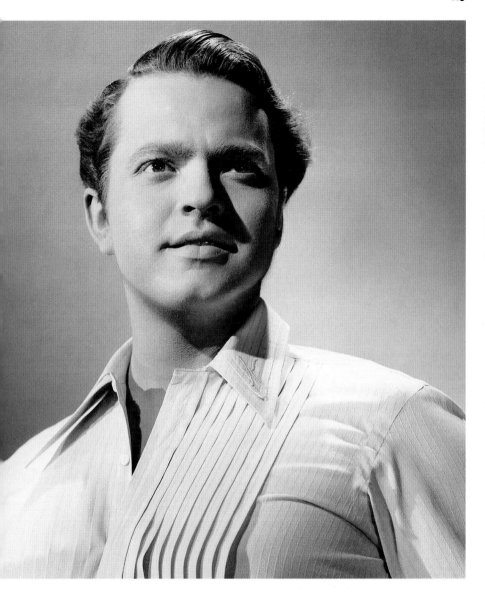

PORTRAIT FROM 'CITIZEN KANE' (1941)
Orson Welles, 1915–1985. Ever young, ever the dreamer
and doer. / Orson Welles, 1915–1985. Immer jung, immer
der Träumer und der Macher. / Orson Welles, 1915–1985.
Éternellement jeune, éternel rêveur toujours en action.

ANTHONY PERKINS en

EL PROCESO

SEGUN LA NOVELA DE
KAFKA

con

JEANNE MOREAU
ELSA MARTINELLI
ROMY SCHNEIDER
AKIM TAMIROFF
MADELEINE ROBINSON
ORSON WELLES
DIRECTOR:
ORSON WELLES

JANO.

4

FILMOGRAPHY

FILMOGRAFIE

FILMOGRAPHIE

FILMS AS DIRECTOR/SPIELFILME ALS REGISSEUR/ORSON WELLES RÉALISATEUR

Citizen Kane (1941)

The Magnificent Ambersons/Der Glanz des Hauses Amberson/La Splendeur des Amberson (1942)

Journey into Fear/Von Agenten gejagt/Voyage au pays de la peur (1942) co-directed with Norman Foster/ Co-Regie mit Norman Foster/coréalisé avec Norman Foster; uncredited/nicht genannt/non crédité

The Stranger/Der Fremde/Le Criminel (1946)

The Lady from Shanghai/Die Lady von Shanghai/La Dame de Shanghaï (1948)

Macbeth (1948)

Othello/Othello/Orson Welles' Othello (1952)

Mr Arkadin (Confidential Report)/Herr Satan persönlich/Dossier secret (1955)

Touch of Evil/Im Zeichen des Bösen/La Soif du mal (1958)

The Trial/Der Prozeß/Le Procès (1962)

Chimes at Midnight/Falstaff/Falstaff (1966)

The Immortal Story/Stunde der Wahrheit/Une histoire immortelle (1968)

F for Fake/F wie Fälschung/Vérité et mensonges (1974)

Filming 'Othello' (1979)

DIRECTED FOR TELEVISION/FERNSEH-REGIE/RÉALISATIONS POUR LA TÉLÉVISION

The Sketchbook of Orson Welles (BBC, 1955)

The Fountain of Youth (1956–58)

UNFINISHED FEATURE FILMS/ UNVOLLENDETE SPIELFILME/ LONGS MÉTRAGES INACHEVÉS

It's All True (1942) A documentary including extant sections was released in 1993./Ein Dokumentarfilm mit existierenden Fragmenten erschien 1993./Un documentaire comprenant les portions subsistantes est sorti en 1993.

Don Quixote (1955-73) An edited version by Jess Franco was released in 1992./Eine geschnittene Fassung von Jess Franco kam 1992 heraus heraus [als *Don Quijote de Orson Welles*]./Une version remaniée par Jess Franco a paru en 1992.

The Deep (1967-69)

The Merchant of Venice/Der Kaufmann von Venedig/Le Marchand de Venise (1969)

The Other Side of the Wind (1970-76)

The Dreamers (1980-82) only 20 finished minutes existant/Es existieren nur 20 fertig gestellte Minuten./Seule une portion achevée de 20 minutes a été conservée.

FILMS AS ACTOR ONLY/SPIELFILME ALS SCHAUSPIELER/ORSON WELLES ACTEUR

Jane Eyre/Die Waise von Lowood/Jane Eyre (1943)

Follow the Boys/Follow the Boys/Hollywood Parade (1944)

Tomorrow is Forever/Morgen ist die Ewigkeit/ Demain viendra toujours (1945)

Duel in the Sun/Duell in der Sonne/Duel au soleil (1947) as narrator/als Erzähler/narrateur

Black Magic/Schwarze Magie/Cagliostro (1947)

Prince of Foxes/In den Klauen des Borgia/Échec à Borgia (1948)

The Third Man/Der dritte Mann/Le Troisième Homme (1949)

The Black Rose/Die schwarze Rose/La Rose noire (1950)

Return to Glennascaul/Rückkehr nach Glennascaul/Retour à Glennascaul (1951)

Trent's Last Case/Trents letzter Fall/L'Affaire Manderson (1953)

Royal Affairs in Versailles/Wenn Versailles erzählen könnte/Si Versailles m'était conté ... (1953)

Man, Beast and Virtue/Man, Beast and Virtue/ L'Homme, la bête et la vertu (1953)

Napoleon/Napoleon/Napoléon (1954)

Trouble in the Glen/Scherereien mit seiner Lordschaft/Révolte dans la vallée (1954)

Three Cases of Murder/Mord ohne Mörder/Trois meurtres (1955)

Moby Dick (1956)

Man in the Shadow/Des Teufels Lohn/Le Salaire du diable (1957)

The Long Hot Summer/Der lange heiße Sommer/ Les Feux de l'été (1957)

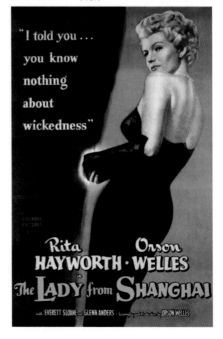

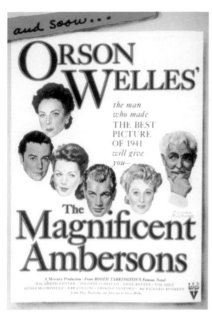

The Roots of Heaven/Die Wurzeln des Himmels/
Les Racines du ciel (1958)

The Vikings/Die Wikinger/Les Vikings (1958)
as narrator/ als Erzähler/narrateur

Compulsion/Der Zwang zum Bösen/Le Génie du
mal (1959)

David and Goliath/David und Goliath/David et
Goliath (1959)

Ferry to Hong Kong/Fähre nach Hongkong/Visa
pour Hong-Kong (1959)

Austerlitz (1960)

Crack in the Mirror/Drama im Spiegel/Drame
dans un miroir (1960)

The Tartars/Die Tartaren/Les Tartares (1961)

King of Kings/König der Könige/Le Roi des rois
(1961) as narrator/als Erzähler/narrateur

Lafayette/Lafayette/La Fayette (1961)

The VIP's/Hotel International/Hôtel international
(1963)

RoGoPag (1963)

The Fabulous Adventures of Marco Polo/Im Reich
des Kublai Khan/La Fabuleuse Aventure de Marco
Polo (1964)

Is Paris Burning?/Brennt Paris?/Paris brûle-t-il ?
(1966)

A Man For All Seasons/Ein Mann zu jeder
Jahreszeit/Un homme pour l'éternité (1966)

Casino Royale (1967)

The Sailor from Gibraltar/Nur eine Frau an Bord/
Le Marin de Gibraltar (1967)

I'll Never Forget What's 'Isname/Was kommt
danach ...?/Qu'arrivera-t-il après ? (1967)

Oedipus the King/König Ödipus/Œdipe roi
(1968)

House of Cards/Jedes Kartenhaus zerbricht/Un cri
dans l'ombre (1968)

Tepepa (Blood and guns/Long Live the Revolution)/
Tepepa (Durch die Hölle, Compañeros/Der
Eliminator)/Trois pour un massacre (1968)

The Last Roman/Kampf um Rom/Le Dernier des
Romains (1969)

The Southern Star/Der Stern des Südens/L'Étoile
du sud (1969)

The Battle of Neretva/Die Schlacht an der
Neretva/La Bataille de la Neretva (1969)

The Kremlin Letter/Der Brief an den Kreml/La
Lettre du Kremlin (1970)

Start the Revolution Without Me/Die Französische
Revolution fand nicht statt (Zwei Haudegen
kommen selten allein)/Commencez la révolution
sans nous (1970)

12 + 1/Zwölf plus eins/Douze et un (1970)

Catch-22/Catch-22 – Der böse Trick/Catch-22
(1970)

Upon This Rock (1970)

Waterloo (1970)

A Safe Place/Ein Zauberer an meiner Seite/Un coin tranquille (1971)

Ten Days' Wonder/Der zehnte Tag/La Décade prodigieuse (1971)

Malpertuis (1972)

Get to Know Your Rabbit/Hilfe, ich habe Erfolg!/Attention au lapin (1972)

Necromancy (The Witching/Rosemary's Disciples/The Toy Factory/Horror Attack)/Necromancy/Necromancy (1972)

Treasure Island/Die Schatzinsel/L'Île au trésor (1972)

And Then There Were None/Zehn kleine Negerlein/ Dix petits nègres (1974)

Voyage of the Damned/Reise der Verdammten/ Le Voyage des damnés (1976)

A Woman called Moses (1978)

The Double McGuffin/The Double McGuffin/The Double McGuffin (1979) as himself/als er selbst/dans son propre rôle

Blood and Guns/Blood and Guns/Blood and Guns (1979)

The Muppet Movie/Muppet Movie/Les Muppets, ça c'est du cinéma (1979)

Going For Broke (Never Trust an Honest Thief)/ Going For Broke/Going For Broke (1980)

The Secret of Nikola Tesla/The Secret of Nikola Tesla/Le Secret de Nikola Tesla (1980)

History of the World - Part I/Mel Brooks - Die verrückte Geschichte der Welt/La Folle Histoire du monde (1980) as narrator/als Erzähler/narrateur

Butterfly/Der blonde Schmetterling/Butterfly (1981)

The Man Who Saw Tomorrow (1981) as host and narrator/als Präsentator und Erzähler/ présentateur et narrateur.

The Orson Welles Story (1982) BBC documentary; as himself/BBC-Dokumentation; als er selbst/ documentaire de la BBC ; dans son propre rôle

Slapstick of Another Kind (1984) as narrator/als Erzähler/narrateur

Where is Parsifal?/Himmelsmaschine/Where is Parsifal? (1984)

The Transformers/Transformers: Der Film/Les Transformers (1986)

Someone to Love/Ein Tag für die Liebe/Someone to Love (1987)

BIBLIOGRAPHY

WRITTEN BY ORSON WELLES

Welles, Orson with Kodar, Oja, Rosenbaum, Jonathan (Ed.): *The Big Brass Ring, An Original Screenplay.* Santa Teresa Press, 1987.
Welles, Orson, Pepper, James (Ed. & introduction): *The Cradle Will Rock, An Original Screenplay.* Santa Teresa Press, 1994.
Welles, Orson, Bridget Gellert Lyons (Ed.): *Chimes at Midnight.* Rutgers University Press, 1988.
Welles, Orson, Callow, Simon (afterword): *Les Bravades, A Gift for his Daughter.* Workman Publishing, 1996.
Welles, Orson: *Mr Arkadin.* W.H. Allen, 1956.
Welles, Orson, with Bogdanovich, Peter; Rosenbaum, Jonathan (Ed.): *This is Orson Welles.* HarperCollins, 1992.
Welles, Orson; Comito, Terry (Ed.): *Touch of Evil.* Rutgers University Press, 1985.

BIOGRAPHIES, MEMOIRS, ANALYSIS

Andregg, Michael: *Orson Welles, Shakespeare and Popular Culture.* Columbia University Press, 1999.
Bessy, Maurice: *Orson Welles.* Translated from the French by Ciba Vaughan, Crown, 1971.
Bazin, André: *Orson Welles, A Critical View.* Foreword by François Truffaut, profile by Jean Cocteau, Harper & Row, 1978.
Brady, Frank: *Citizen Welles.* Charles Scribner, 1989.
Beja, Morris: *Perspectives on Orson Welles.* G.K. Hall, 1995.
Cantril, Hadley: *Invasion from Mars.* Princeton University Press, 1940.
Carringer, Robert L.: *The Making of Citizen Kane.* University of California Press, 1985.
Carringer, Robert L.: *The Magnificent Ambersons: A Reconstruction.* University of California Press, 1993.
Callow, Simon: *The Road to Xanadu.* Jonathan Cape, 1995.

Cowie, Peter: *A Ribbon of Dreams, The Cinema of Orson Welles.* A.S. Barnes, 1973.
Estrin, Mark W. (Ed.): *Orson Welles Interviews.* University of Mississippi Press, 2002.
Fitzgerald, Martin: *Orson Welles.* Pocket Essentials, 2000.
France, Richard: *The Theater of Orson Welles.* Associated University Presses, 1977.
France, Richard (Ed.): *Orson Welles on Shakespeare: The WPA and the Mercury Theatre Playscripts.* Greenwood Press, 1990.
Higham, Charles: *The Films of Orson Welles.* University of California Press, 1970.
Higham, Charles: *Orson Welles: The Rise and Fall of an American Genius.* St. Martin's Press, 1985.
Houseman, John: *Run-Through.* Simon & Schuster, 1972.
Kael, Pauline: *The Citizen Kane Book.* Kael's essay, *Raising Kane*, marred by shoddy scholarship, prefaces the script by Orson Welles and Herman J. Mankiewicz. Little, Brown, 1971.
Kael, Pauline: *Kiss Kiss Bang Bang.* Contains her positive reviews of *Chimes at Midnight* and *Citizen Kane*, Little, Brown, 1968.
Koch, Howard: *The Panic Broadcast, Portrait of an Event.* Little, Brown, 1970.
Leaming, Barbara: *Orson Welles.* Viking, 1985.
MacLiammoir, Micheal: *Put Money in Thy Purse: The Making of Othello.* Methuen, 1952.
McBride, Joseph: *Orson Welles.* Da Capo, 1996.
Mulvey, Laura: *Citizen Kane.* British Film Institute, 1993.
Naremore, James: *The Magic World of Orson Welles.* Southern Methodist University Press, 1989.
Thomson, David: *Rosebud.* Alfred A. Knopf, 1996.
Wald, Malvin: *Encounter with Orson.* (One-act play, unpublished. Written circa 1998.)
Wood, Bret: *Orson Welles: A Bio-Bibliography.* Greenwood Press, 1990.

IMPRINT

© 2006 TASCHEN GmbH
Hohenzollernring 53, D-50672 Köln
www.taschen.com

Editor/Picture Research: Paul Duncan/Wordsmith Solutions
Editorial Coordination: Martin Holz, Cologne
Production Coordination: Nadia Najm and Horst Neuzner, Cologne
German translation: Thomas J. Kinne, Nauheim
French translation: Anne Le Bot, Paris
Multilingual production: www.arnaudbriand.com, Paris
Typeface Design: Sense/Net, Andy Disl and Birgit Reber, Cologne

Printed in Italy
ISBN-13: 978-3-8228-2003-2
ISBN-10: 3-8228-2003-2

To stay informed about upcoming TASCHEN titles, please request our magazine at www.taschen.com/magazine or write to TASCHEN, Hohenzollernring 53, D-50672 Cologne, Germany, contact@taschen.com, Fax: +49-221-254919. We will be happy to send you a free copy of our magazine which is filled with information about all of our books.